PERSONAL
INTERPRETATION

connecting your audience
to heritage resources

lisa
BROCHU

tim
MERRIMAN

interpPress

NAI is a private nonprofit [501(c)3] organization
and professional association. NAI's mission is:
"Inspiring leadership and excellence to advance
natural and cultural interpretation as a profession."
For information: www.interpnet.com.

ISBN 1-879931-06-0

Printed in Singapore.

For our children

Travis and Trevor
—Lisa

Tobias and Evonne
—Tim

who make our lives
more meaningful.

CONTENTS

FOREWORD

Interpretation is both an old tradition and a new science. There have always been storytellers, interpreters of human culture and natural phenomena, telling the stories of places and people. Those of us who have chosen interpretation as a profession are joining an ancient and honorable tribe that includes shamans, poets, historians, and philosophers as well as John Muir, Enos Mills, and Freeman Tilden, the traditional "fathers" of interpretation.

In another sense, interpretation is a rather young science. Only in the last several decades have books appeared that set out the principles and theory of interpretation, as well as practical suggestions to use in the field. At the same time, our professional association, the National Association for Interpretation (NAI), has been growing and developing ways to help our members strive for interpretive excellence.

I see *Personal Interpretation,* the first book to be published by NAI's new press, InterpPress, as an important step in this journey toward excellence. My friends and colleagues Lisa Brochu and Tim Merriman have written this book as a result of their work developing NAI's Certification Program. It is a synthesis of the best thinking on giving personal interpretive programs from many sources, including the National Park Service, Dave Dahlen, David Larsen, Sam Ham, William Lewis, Joseph Cornell, Ted Cable, Doug Knudson, and Larry Beck.

By gathering in one place the basics of personal interpretation, this book will be invaluable for anyone new to the field, from docents and educators in museums, zoos, and aquaria, to front-line interpreters in parks, nature centers, and living-history sites. It is also a great refresher for those of us who are seasoned interpreters looking to renew our dedication to providing the best interpretive programs for the visitors to our sites.

Let me thank the authors for helping NAI members and others continue their quest for excellence in interpretation. As interpreters, we have an important mission. It is through interpretation that we make vital connections with our visitors that take them beyond simply caring about our cultural and natural resources to becoming stewards of those resources.

Sarah D. Blodgett
President
National Association for Interpretation
August 15, 2002

PREFACE

The Story Behind the Book

When Freeman Tilden wrote, "Interpretation is an art; any art is to some degree teachable," he suggested a wonderful opportunity. Interpreters can study their art through social science research, apply what they learn, and provide a scientific basis for improving their craft. And yet the application of science does not limit creativity. In a way, it allows them to focus their creative efforts in a more efficient manner, when they know what is likely to work and what will not.

This book was inspired by our involvement in development of a certification program for the National Association for Interpretation (NAI) between 1997 and 2000. Lisa Brochu served as the chair of the Certification Task Force that developed the first four categories of professional certification: Certified Heritage Interpreter, Certified Interpretive Manager, Certified Interpretive Planner, and Certified Interpretive Trainer. Tim Merriman, as executive director of NAI, developed the first Certified Interpretive Guide training course in 2000 after extensive study of other training courses being delivered in the United States. Brochu then improved the curriculum by writing the first workbook and instructional materials for the course in collaboration with Merriman. Those early efforts were tested with a variety of interpretive guides and interpreters to refine the approach. The result has been the development of an "NAI approach" to personal interpretation that combines what we consider to be the best practices from a number of sources.

Through the process, it became evident that a resource was needed to pull together the principles and fundamentals of personal interpretation expressed by various authors and agencies over many years. This book is not intended as a single source for the profession; nor is it intended to replace or compete with the other excellent resources that currently exist. Instead, it serves as a bridge to those resources by exposing the reader to the variety of materials available. In this book, we will introduce you to Enos Mills, Freeman Tilden, William Lewis, Sam Ham, Douglas Knudson, Larry Beck, Ted Cable, Michael Gross, Ron Zimmerman, and other respected authors in this field.

This book has been organized by chapters that roughly correspond to the material presented in NAI's Certified Interpretive Guide course. To use this book most effectively, we recommend that you maintain a companion library of reference books that includes:

Environmental Interpretation: A Practical Guide, by Sam Ham (1992)
Interpretation of Cultural and Natural Resources, by Knudson, Cable, and Beck (1995)

Interpreting for Park Visitors, by William Lewis (1995, 8th printing)
Interpretation for the 21st Century, by Larry Beck and Ted Cable (1998)
Interpreting Our Heritage, by Freeman Tilden (1957)
Sharing Nature with Children, by Joseph Cornell (1998, 2nd edition)

Each of these books goes into far more depth on the subject areas covered in this book and should be referred to often as you continue to develop your interpretive career skills. They are the primary sources for much of the material in this book and contain the research that supports the principles of interpretive behavior. We strongly encourage you to begin your library with the aforementioned books as a foundation, then continue to add other titles appropriate to your interpretive interests.

We also recommend that you visit the National Park Service's Interpretive Development Program web site (www.nps.gov/idp/interp). There you'll find content outlines, references, and resources used by the National Park Service's competency program. Many of the key features of the interpretive approach in this book were inspired by materials of the National Park Service, which has been and continues to be a significant contributor to and resource for the profession.

Following each chapter in this book, specific reading materials related to the subject covered in that chapter are listed, many of which come from the six books listed above. We hope that this approach will help point you in the right direction for additional information.

This book is about personal interpretation, the craft of the interpretive professional who provides face-to-face programs for the public. Whether the job title is guide, docent, ranger, naturalist, historian, cruise director, or interpreter, the process of program development and delivery is essentially the same. This book is intended as a starting point for any heritage interpreter seeking knowledge of the fundamentals of the field. It does not, however, address the broad scope of non-personal interpretive media (signs, brochures, exhibits).

We have written around the assumption that *interpretation must add value to achieving the mission of the organization.* If we seem to be shouting that, it is for a simple reason. Some interpretive programming has been developed solely out of the personal interests and skills of the individuals interpreting the resources without any connection to management of the parent organization. Invariably these programs are eliminated in lean financial times. They are viewed correctly as icing on a cake, tasty but not essential. We believe that well-applied personal interpretation is the cake. It is nourishing, valuable, and the most cost-efficient way to manage our resources.

When interpreters help people understand the wonderful natural and cultural heritage stories of the world, they enlist wholehearted support in protecting those resources and communicating vital stories to others whom they will never see. Nothing is more powerful than voluntary compliance, for an understanding public helps to keep everyone engaged in more thoughtful uses of resources. At the heart of this understanding is you, the guide, the interpreter. You must understand the power of interpretive communication and apply it thoughtfully and strategically. To do this effectively, you must know what others before you have learned and how to apply the knowledge they can share.

And so, we offer this book, designed as a starting place for newly hired interpreters, seasonal interpreters, volunteers, and docents who will be practicing personal interpretation. It can also serve as a refresher for someone who returns to interpretation after doing other work. It provides the bare essentials of what an interpreter should know, but it is by no means everything you need to know to do your best job.

Any profession that grows and matures must continually study its own work and base improvements on measurable change. We provide only a glimpse of the social science research and want you to use the broader textbooks to continue your education.

The Semantics of Interpretation

We hope this book will be used by anyone and everyone who is involved in preparing or presenting personal interpretation programs. We recognize that covers a broad spectrum of individuals, interests, and organizational structures. The more people who reviewed the book prior to publication, the more comments we received about using specific words like *audience* as opposed to *guests* or *customers,* or *themes* as opposed to *main ideas,* or *guides* as opposed to *interpreters.* We've tried to be sensitive to the fact that there are different ways of looking at our profession and those we serve. We use some terms (such as those mentioned above) somewhat interchangeably and hope that our readers will keep an open mind, mentally adjusting specific terminology as they read along to suit the needs of their own individual or organizational interests.

Lisa Brochu and Tim Merriman

ACKNOWLEDGMENTS

The fine work of many colleagues built the solid foundation for this book. Enos Mills and Freeman Tilden wrote classics with their books *Adventures of a Nature Guide* and *Interpreting Our Heritage,* respectively. We continue to quote them and expect their original ideas to be inspirational into the future. Bill Lewis's book, *Interpreting for Park Visitors,* contains practical ideas for connecting with people in parks, and his thoughts are worth repeating to every young interpreter. Sam Ham's solid work in *Environmental Interpretation: A Practical Guide for People with Big Ideas and Small Budgets* has been and will continue to be a source of inspiration and usable ideas for generations of interpreters. We quote Ham profusely for he brought social science research and interpretive practices together in a very practical way. Douglas Knudson, Larry Beck, and Ted Cable's text, *Interpretation of Cultural and Natural History,* documents the many research works that support the field. Larry Beck and Ted Cable's *Interpretation for the 21st Century* introduced some other stimulating ideas in their update of Tilden's six principles.

We owe a special debt of gratitude to the National Park Service (NPS) and Mather Training Center. Corky Mayo, Mike Watson, Dave Dahlen, David Larsen, and hundreds of NPS interpreters invested their talents and resources in the Interpretive Development Program (IDP) and development of interpretive competencies. The IDP contributed many wonderful ideas and activities that we have shared with the entire interpretive profession through this book and NAI's certification and training program.

There are many other fine texts and resources in the interpretive field, and their omission here is in no way due to any deficiency on their part. The above-named individuals and their resources have simply been the most important in preparing this text. We also wish to thank K.C. DenDooven for his thoughtful support, encouragement, and technical advice. We hope you find this book useful and that you choose to share your ideas in future articles, books, and workshops. We all learn more when we share with each other.

Lisa Brochu and Tim Merriman

Overview of Interpretive Profession

Prior to Gutenberg's invention of the printing press, the average person relied on the human gift of speech to transfer values, skills, and ideas from generation to generation. Learning from elders, shamans, medicine men and women, and priests or priestesses was highly valued. These most experienced tribal members selected what was most important to teach a youngster. In China, persons who reached the age of ninety were believed to be so wise from experience that they could advise even the emperor without being offensive. Each decade of age imparted new rights to elders of the tribe (Sinclair, Kevin, and Iris Wong Po-yee. 2002. *Culture Shock.* Portland, OR: Graphic Arts Center Publishing Co.).

Worldwide the history of each tribe and what was known of science was taught around the campfire or by using real tools in a hands-on manner. Lessons were compelling because survival depended upon knowledge of how to make a bow, basket, hoe, or pot. The discomfort of disease or illness could be relieved by knowledge of roots or herbs with healing powers. Evening stories from elders around the campfire created the fabric of a community, woven from threads of truth, myths, ideas, and folklore. They entertained, delivered messages about the tribal history, and had a moral or hidden meaning. The listeners absorbed the meanings through repetition, then would tell the stories themselves as age gave them the wisdom and authority to be heard.

Today's world still relies on interpersonal communication, but modern society, especially in developed nations, teaches about culture in a great many ways— schools, television, radio, the Internet, play, family, and in nonformal settings. Play, family, and nonformal settings have routinely employed firsthand learning,

"A people who have no zeal for knowing their past are unlikely to have a future worth anybody's admiration" (Tilden, Freeman. *The Fifth Essence: An Invitation to Share in Our Eternal Heritage*. Washington, DC: National Park Trust Board). Lincoln Memorial photo by Paul Caputo.

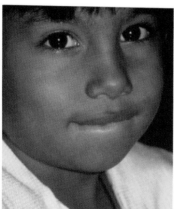

Future generations rely on us for an accurate and fair portrayal of the stories of nature and history. Photo by Gerald Bauer.

Legacy, NAI's bimonthly color magazine, updates guides, interpreters, and administrators on important stories in the profession.

encouraging real contact with the planet's resources, but sadly, that contact is rapidly disappearing. Children who once fought mock battles on their chargers (bicycles) against evil foes (the neighbor kids), might now be pitted against the talents of a game inventor who entertains the child with a joy stick and a computer monitor or game screen. Parents who once asked their children to mow the lawn, paint the fence, and feed the pets or livestock, have given those tasks over to contractors. Children often leave home for college or work with little hands-on experience to face the nature of real-life dilemmas.

The recreational settings of nature centers, zoos, museums, parks, historic sites, and aquaria now become more important because they put children and adults back in contact with the real resource, not an electronic or print image of it. Are the interpreters of those resources the "elders" with the wisdom to teach the skills and tell the stories that transfer their culture? To some extent, the answer is yes. Interpreters do have tremendous power they may not realize. Because people tend to believe what interpreters tell them to a greater degree than they might believe what they read in books, it matters a great deal that interpreters have personal integrity about what they do. Their audience is relying on their honesty. The employer is depending upon thoughtful efforts to achieve organizational goals and objectives. Everyone expects the interpreter to be a professional in every sense of the word.

Interpretation as a Profession

We often say or hear colleagues say we are "professionals." It's important that interpreters understand the responsibilities that go with that descriptor. Interpreters need to ask the question: "What makes a profession?" Answers include:

- Public service with social responsibility
- Foundation of knowledge—research-based
- Specialized education and training
- Responsibility on practitioners
- Programs of accreditation and certification
- Established codes of ethics
- Lifelong learning

Interpreters or guides help audiences make connections with history, culture, science, and the special places on the planet. The informality of the setting makes it easy to forget that interpreters handle a very sacred trust—the stories of where humankind has been, who we are, and what we have learned. And interpreters do it with real things, real places, and often with the intimacy of talking one on one.

Interpreters have a social responsibility to be accurate and fair in their depiction of peoples and their stories. At a Civil War site, the audience includes people who identify with the stories of opposing sides. How can interpreters be accurate and fair, presenting the passion of both sides who fought and died for their beliefs? The interpreter has to know enough about the whole story to deliver it with balance and respect for the varied points of view of those who fought in that most critical war in American history, in which families were split by the divisiveness of issues.

Social science research teaches that interpretation is both art and science. As the foundation of research-based knowledge expands, we improve our training and teaching about the interpretive profession. Each generation of interpreters advances the work of those who came before, expanding not only the science but enlarging the art. As Freeman Tilden, author of *Interpreting Our Heritage* (1957), encouraged, "C'est l'homme." It is the person and her or his personal style and passion that brings unique value to the messages delivered and how they are received. Interpreters have to understand that power and use it responsibly. Interpreters are not there to propagandize, but to reveal important stories behind the resources so that audience members can formulate their own opinions and take responsibility for their actions.

Every interpreter has a personal responsibility to research carefully the messages being conveyed, to represent their organizations faithfully, and to handle the facts, artifacts, and stories of culture and science ethically. Because interpreters affect what people believe about themselves and the world, what they do matters very much. But by the nature of the work, an interpreter's code of ethics must be managed from within him- or herself. The audience and even the organization may not know when the interpreter fails to act ethically. Interpreters, as individuals, must protect the dignity and value of the profession in the careful handling of every activity.

As renowned poet Robert Frost wrote in his poem, "Stopping by Woods on a Snowy Evening," there are "miles to go before we sleep." There is always more to know about the resources to be interpreted, the audiences to be served, or the variety of communication techniques available. The journey of self-improvement in the interpretive profession will never grow old because of this continual effort to change and apply new and innovative ideas. The responsibility to improve belongs to each individual as a professional.

Role of the National Association for Interpretation

Think about King Arthur's mythical court with its visions of bold knights pledging their lives and fealty to the king they admired. Professions arouse that kind of enthusiasm and loyalty. We recognize that we do not just want our own performance to improve. We want all who work in our field to get better and bring the profession up a notch or two. This remarkable desire to improve the profession includes teaching each other and learning from colleagues.

In 1954, about forty naturalists gathered at Bradford Woods in Indiana to meet and discuss common ideas and interests. That first networking activity led to the formation of the Association of Interpretive Naturalists (AIN). In the mid-1960s a group of heritage interpreters in California gathered to form the Western Interpreters Association (WIA). Many of them were cultural interpreters as well as naturalists, and the WIA name reflected that broader interest. These two professional organizations served their respective members (many of whom belonged to both organizations) for several decades before consolidating in 1988 to form the National Association for Interpretation (NAI). The headquarters of the newly consolidated association was moved to Fort Collins, Colorado, to affiliate with Colorado State University (CSU) and the Natural Resources Recreation and Tourism Department, which has had a strong undergraduate and graduate program in interpretation for several decades.

For about eight years, the NAI headquarters was housed in the Forestry Building on the CSU campus. In 1995, NAI purchased an 1898 Victorian brick house at 528 South Howes and moved into new quarters just a block from the CSU campus.

NAI maintains a full-time staff of six and a part-time staff of eight. As of the year 2001, more than forty-five hundred members of the association in all fifty of the United States and in thirty nations, are taking part in NAI's networking and training activities. Members can elect to participate on a national or international level, regionally, and within special-interest sections. Training workshops with something of interest to everyone are held throughout the country at different times of the year. They include:

- National Interpreters Workshop (NIW), an annual fall training/networking event
- Western Regional Interpretive Skills Training (WRIST), an annual June event
- Interpretive Management Institute (IMI), an annual management training event
- Regional workshops and sectional workshops, annual events
- Certification workshops, ongoing

Written resources are also an important part of the membership services that support sharing among professionals. NAI's major written resources include:

- *Legacy* magazine, published six times per year
- *Journal of Interpretation Research,* published semi-annually
- *Jobs in Interpretation* newsletter, published semi-monthly
- *InterpNews* newsletter, published quarterly
- Ten regional and eleven sectional newsletters
- InterpNet web site—http://www.interpnet.com

NAI also offers an Association Store to supply professional books and NAI logo apparel at discount rates to members. All of these products, programs, and services support NAI's stated mission: "Inspiring leadership and excellence to advance natural and cultural interpretation as a profession."

NAI's Certification Program

In 1998, NAI began offering certification services in four categories to support the organization's mission of advancing interpretation as a profession. These categories are Certified Heritage Interpreter (CHI), Certified Interpretive Manager (CIM), Certified Interpretive Trainer (CIT), and Certified Interpretive Planner

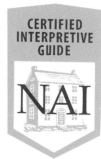

Guides earn the coveted Certified Interpretive Guide credential by demonstrating mastery of presentational skills.

Interpreters at Walt Disney World's Animal Kingdom create safe interactions between animals and children on Discovery Island. Photo by Tim Merriman.

(CIP). In 2000, the Certified Interpretive Guide (CIG) category was added to these services. One way to demonstrate your knowledge of interpretation and ability to apply interpretive principles is to become certified in one or more of these categories. Though it does not guarantee professional employment, it gives you credibility recognized by the entire profession and can make it easier to be hired or get promotions.

The CHI, CIT, CIM, and CIP professional categories are designed to recognize existing skills and knowledge gained through academic studies or experience. These categories require a minimum of a bachelor's degree or four years of experience or some equivalent combination of education and experience to apply. Additional information about the requirements for these categories can be found in the *Certification Handbook and Study Guide,* available as a downloadable file from the NAI web site or from the NAI headquarters.

The Certified Interpretive Guide (CIG) category was designed as a training program for those who interpret nature or history with the public but have not had the benefit of an academic background or prior experience in the field. Typical CIG candidates might be volunteers, docents, temporary staff, seasonal employees, or new full-time interpreters or guides who lead tours or conduct programs.

To become a CIG, you must be at least sixteen years old and take a thirty-two-hour CIG course offered by an NAI-sanctioned trainer. On the last of the course's four days, you must make a ten-minute thematic presentation

More than two thousand National Park Service interpreters and guides share the stories of our nation's natural and cultural heritage. Photo by Tim Merriman.

and attain a score of 80 percent or better. You also must submit an outline of your presentation and pass a fifty-question objective exam. A grade of 80 percent on each of those items is also required. The CIG credential you earn is valid for four years. To renew your CIG credential, you must demonstrate that you have had at least forty hours of additional training related to interpretation during the previous four years and pay a re-certification fee to NAI. Certified Interpretive Guides may use the letters CIG after their names on professional correspondence and the CIG logo on ads or brochures used to solicit business.

It is possible to upgrade your CIG credential to a CHI (or other professional category) credential once you have fulfilled the minimum CHI experience or education requirement. The objective exam is the same for all five categories, and once it is taken and passed in any category, it is not necessary to take it again. However, all other requirements must still be met for any other categories you may choose to attain. These requirements, which differ slightly in content for each of the four categories, include completion of an essay exam and up to four evidences of performance. All requirements must be passed with at least an 80 percent score.

It is possible to hold a credential in more than one category at a time. All categories are valid for four years after the date of certification and must be renewed with proof of at least forty hours of continued training from any appropriate source (college course, professional organization, private contractor, in-house agency).

Jobs in Interpretation
Government

Imagine standing in front of Old Faithful, the famed geyser at Yellowstone, America's oldest national park. There's a group of families in front of you, delighted with the bubbling of the thermal pools. You pick up on their interest and use it to explain plate tectonics and volcanic forces at work within the planet. Then right on cue, Old Faithful erupts, providing a visceral experience that seals the memory of what you've just said into their hearts and minds forever. That's just one example of thousands of interpretive opportunities at public parks, nature centers, zoos, botanic gardens, museums, forests, and historic sites.

Almost since its inception in 1916, the U.S. National Park Service (NPS) has led the way among public sector agencies as interpreters of nature and history. At the beginning of the twenty-first century, more than two thousand employees of NPS worked as interpreters or support personnel at nearly four hundred sites comprising more than eighty million acres. Nearly 170,000 volunteers and docents also work in national parks, monuments, and historic sites in an interpretive role. Far and away, NPS is the largest single employer of interpreters, paid and nonpaid.

Interpretive services are available through most other federal agencies that manage natural and cultural resources. These include the USDA Forest Service, U.S. Bureau of Land Management, U.S. Army Corps of Engineers, and U.S. Fish and Wildlife Service. To a lesser degree, the National Oceanic and Atmospheric Administration, the National Aeronautics and Space Administration, the U.S. Geological Survey, and the U.S. Environmental Protection Agency are involved in environmental education and interpretation, often through development of curricula, maps, and publications.

State, county, and municipal agencies operating zoos, museums, historic sites, aquaria, and nature centers also employ guides and interpreters. It is difficult to say how many interpretive professionals are employed in the United States, but it is fair to say that the number of public-sector interpreters is in the thousands. Seasonal interpreters are the major front-line work force in many of these agencies. Some interpreters work opposing seasons with different organizations. It's possible to have a summer seasonal job in Alaska and work the winter tourist season at a park in Florida or Arizona. Many full-time professional interpreters and guides start their careers in these seasonal positions and work them year-round until they find full-time positions.

Nongovernmental Organizations (NGOs)
Not-for-profit. Many not-for-profit nature centers, zoos, museums, aquaria, and historic sites employ interpreters or interpretive guides. Sometimes the interpreter or guide trains volunteers and docents to deliver programs. Many interpreters and guides with not-for-profit organizations work closely with school systems to provide environmental education programs. Sometimes these are outreach programs performed at the schools and in classrooms. In other circumstances, the programs

may involve field trips to the nature center, zoo, or museum. Some interpreters find employment with residential camps or experiential education programs like Outward Bound.

For-profit. Futurist John Naisbitt wrote in *Global Paradox* in 1994 (New York: William Morrow and Company) that one out of every nine people on the planet works in travel and tourism. Interpreters and guides who work for these for-profit companies may not be called by that name, but the job is essentially an interpretive job. Many tour companies use interpretation to add value to the travel experience.

Cruise directors are usually the guides or interpreters for cruise companies. You might work on a boat that takes day trips to watch whales or on a cruise boat that takes longer trips to Baja California, or up the inland passage from Seattle, Washington, to Juneau, Alaska. Bus drivers often take on double duty as the interpreters with long-distance or land-based tour companies. Trekking companies or cultural tour companies employ interpreters to lead their tours and provide a variety of services, from driving the van to general hospitality. As part of their duties, they interpret the areas and people they encounter for their customers.

Some interpreters who gain experience in interpretive writing, exhibit design, and planning become consultants or work for consultants, assisting organizations and agencies with individual interpretive projects. Although these jobs are often in the area considered nonpersonal interpretation (providing signs, exhibits, and so forth), opportunities also exist for contractual management or presentation of interpretive programs. Entrepreneurial interpreters can also make a living through contracted personal appearances, particularly if they develop a character that appeals to a local, national, or international audience. Television's Bill Nye, "The Science Guy," and John Acorn, "The Nature Nut," are classic examples of combining technical knowledge with innate communication skills to interpret common subjects to a widespread audience. The opportunities for success as an entrepreneurial interpreter are limited only by the creativity and business skills of the individual.

Recommended Reading

Brochu, Lisa, and Tim Merriman. 2000. *NAI Certification Handbook and Study Guide.* Fort Collins, CO: National Association for Interpretation.

Knudson, Douglas M., Ted T. Cable, and Larry Beck. 1995. *Interpretation of Cultural and Natural Resources.* State Park, PA: Venture Publishing, Inc.

History of Interpretation

There must have been people like interpreters in every tribe over hundreds of thousands of years, telling stories and sharing traditions around the campfire. The wondrous fabric of civilization around the world is woven from the science and culture of the people. There has always been too much information to pass along all that is known to each young person, so cultures rely on storytellers to choose what is worthy of transmission to future generations. Sometimes these stories are personal favorites of the storytellers, but at times the church, king, or other leaders have dictated the stories to be told.

The interpretive profession as practiced today is similar to what has been done in the past. Interpreters share many of the same treasured stories and crafts, and deliver new ones. As understanding of nature and history evolves, people teach their natural and cultural heritage to ensure that civilization will continue to change and improve. A few special people have been pathfinders and guides in our profession. They gave it a name and described how interpretation served to inspire and involve people in wanting to know more.

John Muir

The son of a Scottish immigrant preacher, John Muir grew to become one of the most important spokesmen for the conservation movement of the 1800s in America. As a boy, Muir was raised by a fundamentalist father who was abusive when John did not learn his daily Bible verses or do as he was told. As a young man, Muir was temporarily blinded in an accident. He recovered from the experience with a newfound purpose and drive in life. He wanted to live close to the environment he loved. Much later he would write in *John Muir: To Yosemite and Beyond* (Engberg, Robert, and Donald Wesling, Eds. 1980. Madison: University of Wisconsin Press), "More wild knowledge, less arithmetic and grammar—compulsory education in the form of woodcraft, mountain craft, science at first hand."

Muir helped found the Sierra Club and was primarily responsible for getting Yosemite National Park dedicated as a national park in 1890. Muir wrote, "I will interpret the rocks, learn the language of the flood, storm and the avalanche. I'll acquaint myself with the glaciers and wild gardens, and get as near the heart of the world as I can" (Browning, Peter. 1998. *John Muir: In His Own Words*. Lafayette, CA: Great West Books). He may have been the first to use the word *interpret* to describe this understanding of the heritage of the planet. But his choice of words was not a message about modern interpretation. He was in search of his own understanding of all he had seen.

The example Muir set as an interpreter of the natural world was even more important. He demonstrated the amazing power of interpretation to help people understand and care. He inspired generations of young conservationists to interpret what they saw and felt to others, and we continue to follow his good example.

Enos Mills

In 1884, Enos Mills, a boy of fourteen from Fort Scott, Kansas, moved to Colorado and began building a log cabin near the base of Long's Peak. He later wrote, "All the great happinesses of my life have seemed to center around that little cabin I built in boyhood" (*Adventures of a Nature Guide*. 1920. Friendship, WI: New Past Press, Inc.).

At nineteen years of age, while beachcombing in California, Mills met and became friends with John Muir, the noted naturalist. Muir took Mills camping in Yosemite and told him of his dream of making Yosemite into a national park. Mills heeded advice from Muir to become a skilled observer of nature and then to write about it. Muir also encouraged Mills to become a practiced public speaker, and he did just that. Through the years, Mills observed animals carefully and thoughtfully in the field and became an authority on the wild areas and wildlife near his home. His sixteen books and numerous articles about nature include many that are still valued as extraordinary sources of knowledge about wildlife.

Enos Mills would make more than forty personal trips over the ten-mile trail to the summit of nearby Long's Peak just to practice before leading more than 250 parties to the summit in his career as a nature guide. He helped these visitors discover the beauty in the smallest of wildflowers as well as the grandeur of dramatic glaciers and rock formations. Through their discoveries, they learned that attaining the summit was not the real goal. As Mills put it in *Adventures of a Nature Guide,* "The essence is to travel gracefully rather than to arrive."

Mills also trained others to be guides. *Adventures of a Nature Guide* tells of his experiences and gives guidance to others who lead groups in the outdoors. In it Mills wrote, "The aim is to illuminate and reveal the alluring world outdoors by introducing determining influences and the respondent tendencies. A nature guide is an interpreter of geology, botany, zoology and natural history." He was the first modern writer to identify the role of a guide as an interpreter, someone who translates what is seen and experienced to others with less experience.

Mills died at fifty-two years of age, leaving behind a legacy of observations and ideas still being used today by all who interpret the natural and cultural history of the world. His cabin still stands as a museum and tribute to his incredible works. His daughter, Enda Mills Kiley, has kept his story vibrantly alive for decades through her interpretive work. Enos Mills believed that nature guiding could and should be applied in all manner of locations, not just national parks. According to the Federal Interagency Council on Interpretation, there are more than 350,000 nature guides in the United States and many more throughout the world. His prophecy came true when he wrote in *Adventures of a Nature Guide,* "Ere long nature guiding will be an occupation of honor and distinction. May the tribe increase."

Freeman Tilden

Enos Mills suggested that a nature guide's aim is to "illuminate and reveal." Freeman Tilden picked up the idea of revelation and made it part of his six principles of interpretation. Tilden's 1957 book, *Interpreting Our Heritage,* was the first to set down specific principles and guidelines for interpreters to follow. Though varied authors have added to the wealth of knowledge and ideas in the field, Tilden's book is still one of the most valuable resources in an interpreter's professional library. His observations about the field and six principles made a timeless contribution to the profession.

Tilden took on his study of interpretation late in his career. For most of his life he was a playwright, writer, and publisher. At the request of National Park Service director Conrad L. Wirth, he worked under a grant from the Old Dominion Foundation to study interpretation and write about it in the early 1950s. The Department of Interior's National Park Service (NPS) was his model under requirements of the grant. NPS had been employing rangers as interpreters almost since it began in 1916. Tilden's travels to and studies of national parks and monuments throughout the United States provided examples for his clear expression of ideas about interpretation. His definition of interpretation, published in *Interpreting Our Heritage,* became the standard within the field for four decades. It states that interpretation is "an educational activity which aims to reveal meanings and relationships through the use of original objects, by firsthand experience, and by illustrative media, rather than simply to communicate factual information."

Tilden's suggestion "to reveal meanings and relationships" was further explored in his book *The Fifth Essence: An Invitation to Share in Our Eternal Heritage* (Washington, DC: National Park Trust Board), in which he explained the importance of meanings. He observed that the ancient Greeks considered "earth, air, fire, and water" to be the four essences. He explained that "meanings" or the "soul" is the "fifth essence." Revealing the soul of the resources is a critical component of good interpretation. The meanings behind the resource matter. Agencies set aside parks, collect artifacts, display animals, and build exhibits to reveal meanings. The organizations interpreters represent have a mission. In most cases, the mission states some higher purpose to educate people, protect resources, preserve special places, and help others understand heritage. Interpreting, or revealing meanings, is the method chosen to achieve those purposes.

William Lewis

In an interview published in *Legacy* magazine in 2000, author and professor of interpretation Sam Ham said of William Lewis, "I consider him to be a master of interpretation." With degrees in physics and speech, Lewis has brought unique academic interests to his field. Lewis worked as a seasonal interpreter for the National Park Service for more than three decades. He trained countless young interpreters and guides and was mentor to many young people as a professor at the University of Vermont. His book *Interpreting for Park Visitors* (1980) has been a classic resource for park interpreters and guides right up to the present. Ham credits Lewis with being his inspiration for teaching "thematic interpretation." Lewis points out that he took the approach from the teachings of Aristotle, who emphasized that communication must always convey a central purpose.

Lewis started the first chapter of his book with the statement, "One thing we know for sure is that every one of us sees the world uniquely." This valued observation is still an important part of training about personal interpretation. Audiences come with different experiences and will understand communication from personal perspectives shaped by their experiences. Lewis also observed that "…we bring together a unique interpreter, a unique visitor, and a unique world, all of which are in the process of change." He referred to the interpreter, visitor, and resource as the "interactive threesome." Lewis wrote that "the interpreter must know himself/herself, the park visitor(s), and the park area itself."

Lewis was convinced that content or resource knowledge is not enough. Interpreters must be social scientists as well, learning about the audience, the process of communication, and the perceptions people have of the resources being interpreted. With the aid of psychological knowledge, interpreters can better understand themselves and the motivations of people in general. "How do people learn?" asks Lewis, and how do their learning styles affect their perception of interpretive experiences we craft? Guides, or interpreters, face a lifelong challenge of mastering knowledge of all three elements of the interactive threesome.

Interpreting Under the Influence

If you begin to notice a pattern of authors building on the work of those who have gone before, you're beginning to think like an interpreter and see the linkages that bind us all together. The simple fact is that knowledge is intoxicating, and many fine authors have had influence for good reasons. If you want to grow, there are many places to learn more about applying the principles of interpretation. In Chapter 9, we offer a bibliography that will help you identify some of the key resources in interpretive philosophy. But don't stop there.

Many authors continue to inspire interpreters in a variety of ways. Rachel Carson had a far-reaching impact on the environmental movement, starting in the 1950s and '60s, as an interpretive author who wrote *The Sea Around Us* (1951. Oxford, UK: Oxford University Press), *The Edge of the Sea* (1955. Boston: Houghton Mifflin Co.), and *The Silent Spring* (1962. Boston: Houghton Mifflin Co.). One of the best sources of program ideas is *Reading the Landscape of America* by May Thielgaard Watts (1957. Rochester, NY: Nature Study Guild Publishers). Inspirational writers like Aldo Leopold, Annie Dillard, Barry Lopez, Wallace Stegman, and Terry Tempest Williams provide wonderful ideas, information, and quotes to incorporate in your programming. Michael Gross and Ron Zimmerman have been distinguished as professors and trainers at the University of Wisconsin at Stevens Point for two decades. With other authors they have published a series of handbooks for the more technical aspects of interpretation.

If you have chosen interpretation as a profession, then you are probably a person who likes to read and explore new ideas. As you find a new influence that is useful, take notes that summarize the most important ideas or quotes you come across. Keep those in a journal or on your computer, and they will become a valuable resource.

Defining What We Do

Through the years, the definition of interpretation proposed by Freeman Tilden has been adopted and applied by thousands of interpreters and guides. More recently, Sam Ham wrote in *Environmental Interpretation: A Practical Guide* (1992. Golden, CO: North American Press), "Environmental interpretation involves translating the technical language of a natural science or related field into terms and ideas that people who aren't scientists can readily understand."

Ham's practical statement about the field of environmental interpretation makes the point that translation is involved. The implication is important. If you talk to a person who speaks only Mandarin Chinese, you would recognize that any message you attempt to deliver in English will not be understood. You would quickly adapt to using sign language and pointing at items to communicate with others without the handy use of language.

As Ham suggests in *Environmental Interpretation,* sometimes interpreters are translating "the technical language of a natural science or related field" through interpretation. But sometimes they are trying to explain the unexplainable or interpret the ancient messages left by a carver of petroglyphs or creator of pictographs. Audiences come from many countries, different cultures, and varied backgrounds, so there is more than just a language barrier. Interpreters must translate the meanings inherent in resources to an audience that will only understand what is seen or experienced through their own life-experience filters. Interpreters meet this challenge by understanding the principles of personal interpretation. They learn as much as possible about the audience and the meanings they want to reveal. They carefully craft the messages they want to deliver, and then they apply their skills as interpreters in using appropriate techniques. That is the art of interpretation, putting it all together to help people make emotional and intellectual connections, as defined by the National Association for Interpretation.

In their book *Interpretation of Cultural and Natural Resources,* Knudson, Cable, and Beck wrote that "...interpretation is how people communicate the significance of cultural and natural resources. It instills appreciation and understanding." Their book gives an excellent survey of the many other definitions found in professional literature. All of these varied definitions lead to the simple but important question, What do they all have in common?

Finding Common Ground

Most authors of books on interpretation have said, in one way or another, that interpreters deliver messages that connect with the interests of the audiences and reveal meanings. All seem to agree that interpretation is more than information but involves information. Most agree that it is a communication process rather than a product.

In recent years, the National Park Service has devoted considerable time and effort to a discussion of the definitions of interpretation that have evolved over time. Their discussions led to the 1996 development of a base rubric that guides the organization's ten competency assessments. The rubric states the following (from www.nps.gov/idp/interp):

The (product) is:

1) Successful as a catalyst in creating an opportunity for the audience to form their own intellectual and emotional connections with meanings/significance inherent in the resource; and

2) Appropriate for the audience, and provides clear focus for their connection with the resource(s) by demonstrating the cohesive development of a relevant idea or ideas, rather than relying primarily on a recital of a chronological narrative or a series of related facts.

The National Association for Interpretation (NAI) has adopted a definition of interpretation that is very close to that of the NPS rubric. NAI defines interpretation thusly: "Interpretation is a communication process that forges emotional and intellectual connections between the interests of the audience and the inherent meanings in the resource."

NAI's definition is, in spirit and intent, the same as what NPS uses, but it was worded to represent the broader interests of the entire profession. Interpreters work in parks, zoos, museums, nature centers, aquaria, and historic sites. They interpret on cruise boats, trails, city streets, under water, on mountaintops, from canoes, kayaks, trains, ships, buses, and via remote cameras in bat caves or in deep ocean on bathyscapes. The definition for the profession must apply broadly to these many and varied organizations, settings, and situations. Also, NAI wants to be sure that people who practice this profession are reminded to make both emotional and intellectual connections. This is much the same idea as Tilden's statement that interpreters must do more than communicate "factual information." Facts are intellectually interesting but not enough in most cases to make emotional connections. We believe that it is important that professionals find a common language. Toward that end, we will use the NAI definition throughout this book as our foundation.

What Interpretation Is Not

Tilden's original definition of interpretation went further than stating what interpretation is. He also said clearly what interpretation *is not*. It is not simply the communication of facts. Tilden recognized that facts are important in interpretation, but he also pointed out that they are not enough. Even when done well, a recitation of facts leaves the audience to wonder what it all means.

As interpreters, you hold a certain amount of power and influence over what the audience is led to believe. But interpretation is not your personal soapbox. Those of you who interpret nature and history owe your audiences a balanced presentation. Interpretation should not be "interpreganda." The National Park Service's Bob Roney (master interpreter at Yosemite National Park) identifies "interpreganda" as interpretation that:

- Ignores multiple points of view
- Skews facts toward a foregone conclusion
- Oversimplifies facts
- Comes from a perspective that the audience is ignorant
- Communicates in one direction by discouraging dialogue
- Does not allow audience members to have and maintain a personal perspective

Interpreganda demonstrates a lack of respect for the intelligence of the audience and their rights to honest communication from us. If the audience detects that the guide or interpreter is giving a shaded version of the story, they lose respect for the individual and probably for the entire organization.

Good interpretation portrays multiple and equally valid points of view about any given situation. For example, U.S. Civil War battles had at least two distinct factions represented, each with its own point of view. Descendants of the people who gave their lives in those battles will want to hear their stories told in a thoughtful and respectful manner. Sometimes a third or even a fourth perspective is involved when you consider the representation of black soldiers and families with soldiers on opposing sides. Each of these stories must be told in a manner that balances all of them. It takes some effort and a well-prepared presentation, but it can be done.

In any setting, interpreters want audience members to return, to share their enthusiasm for the experience with friends, and to stay longer the next time. People come to an interpretive experience with all of their personal prejudices, beliefs, and political views. Respecting their diverse opinions and beliefs ensures that they will judge the interpretive experience on its own merits, not its support of any partisan view of environmental issues or cultural controversies.

People come to interpretive programs to be entertained, but interpretation is not simply entertainment. People expect to enjoy their experience in a nonformal setting such as a park, zoo, aquarium, or historic site. However, they have also chosen to attend your interpretive experience, which usually suggests that the guests want to learn something, but they don't want the pressure of a formal learning environment as part of their recreational experience. So they are likely to be disappointed if the program is simply "interpretainment," with no content depth. The National Park Service's Bob Roney characterizes "interpretainment" as that which:

- Stereotypes multiple points of view
- Arranges facts around a punch line
- Oversimplifies facts
- Does not believe the audience is truly interested in the resource
- Does not care what the audience thinks

Have you ever watched a movie or documentary that portrayed an animal, such as a wolf or shark, as evil to create dramatic tension? Hollywood has never claimed to be focused on communication integrity. Movies are often made just to entertain and make money for the producers. Interpretive programs, however, have an obligation to entertain within ethical boundaries. How interpreters communicate about wildlife or cultural stories can affect how people will treat animals or other people in the future.

Medical doctors often say, "First do no harm," as part of their ethical credo. Interpreters should have a similar approach to what they do. Giving people a shallow, stereotyped view of rattlesnakes or bats can result in people killing them needlessly. Interpreters should help others develop a balanced view of respecting the real danger of some wildlife species, while simultaneously learning about the importance of those species in the environment. Audience members will make better choices about how to react to a snake or bat if interpretive efforts have been balanced and thoughtful.

It is equally important to be ethical and balanced in presenting historical or cultural stories. How would you like to see your ethnic group or family portrayed as savage, racist, or hateful in an otherwise entertaining program? You know the harm that stereotyping creates. The audience deserves your most careful efforts in telling stories that characterize a culture or family or individual.

Interpretation Does Not Equal Environmental Education
Teachers who understand the interpretive communication process are usually better teachers. They teach with extra effort, helping their students make intellectual and emotional connections instead of simply memorizing facts. You can recall the teachers who made lessons come alive for you by finding relevance to your life.

Kids make candles the way pioneers did while learning about the people who settled the hills of southern Illinois near Giant City State Park. Photo by Tim Merriman.

Banners such as this one at Waimea Valley on Oahu create expectations for "interpretainment." Photo by Lisa Brochu.

Interpretive technique and good teaching have much in common. Teachers who have not had interpretive training benefit from learning the interpretive communication process. Science and environmental educators find interpretive techniques especially helpful because they are usually outside of the classroom, teaching close to the resource, where interpretive communication processes are most effective.

So when children come to a park or a zoo on a field trip, is it an educational activity or a recreational activity? And are those two things mutually exclusive? The answer lies in the intent and the content of the program. It's a fine line to draw but one that should be clearly understood by those who practice either interpretation and environmental education, or both.

We've identified interpretation as "a communication process that forges emotional and intellectual connections between the interests of the audience and the inherent meanings in the resource." While interpretation may contribute to an educational program, environmental education is a part of a larger system with an established curriculum, educational goals, and specific learning objectives. Field trips that have pretrip activities, posttrip activities, and educational elements in the trip itself that tie into the larger environmental education curriculum of the school are educational activities. The presence of a curriculum and careful alignment of field trip objectives with school curriculum objectives categorizes the trip as educational.

Sometimes the teacher is simply taking the children for a fun day outside the school, and the interpretive program provides justification for doing it. Field trips that leave the interpreter to present whatever she or he wishes, without trying to align with a curriculum, are usually considered interpretive programs. Both of these approaches can be of high quality and valuable to the children, but the latter is considered a recreational activity, even though the audience is a captive one. The same people can be involved, but something different is happening. Viewing interpretive experiences as "awareness" activities that lead to education experiences is reasonable, but it does not make interpretive programming the same as environmental education programs outside the classroom.

Environmental education suggests that a curriculum is involved, and it also identifies that the content will relate to the natural environment. Some teachers consider that environmental education will encompass the built or cultural environment as well, but usually environmental or science educators are focused on ecosystems and the biotic components within those systems. Interpretation, on the other hand, can be applied to any resource at all. The process works just as well in the interpretation of a bog, an industry, a historic house, or an artificial environment such as a space vehicle.

Some people are inclined to define any useful experience as educational. That may be true in a generic definition of the word, but teachers and administrators expect educational field trips to work within a curriculum and align with educational objectives to be dubbed "environmental education." Teachers are under increasing pressure for all school activities to align with statewide educational objectives. Understanding this perspective may help you rework interpretive programs into educational programs in certain circumstances where it may be appropriate to do so. If teachers explicitly ask for environmental education programs and you feel equipped to meet their expectations, you may want to ask the following questions to clarify their needs: What are the specific objectives to be achieved on the field trip? What concepts or ideas do you expect us to teach? Do you want a previsit packet with a glossary of terms, activities to do, assigned readings? Do you expect a follow-up packet after the trip that builds on the experience?

Preparation of an environmental education program in a nonformal setting is usually considerably more work because the educational objectives may not be the same as those of your organization. If you make the commitment to work with teachers in this way, you will likely build a solid and lasting relationship with the schools in your area, especially if your program ties into statewide curriculum goals. They appreciate programming that provides diverse activities for their students while aligning with their specific objectives.

Many excellent packaged environmental education curricula exist for application in nonformal settings. Some of them provide specific training and credentials. A few that are worthy of your consideration are:

- Project WILD
- Project Food, Land and People
- Project WET
- Project Learning Tree
- Nature Scope
- Biodiversity Basics
- OBIS
- GEMS
- Eco-Inquiry

For more information about environmental education, we suggest that you contact the North American Association for Environmental Education, 410 Tarvin Road, Rock Spring, GA 30739, 706-764-2926, www.naaee.org.

Recommended Reading
Knudson, Douglas M., Ted T. Cable, and Larry Beck. 1995. *Interpretation of Cultural and Natural Resources.* State College, PA: Venture Publishing, Inc.

Differentiating Personal and Nonpersonal Interpretation

Personal interpretation is just what it sounds like—one person interpreting to another person or persons. If some part of your job involves talking directly with the public, you are working in the area of personal interpretation. You may be presenting formal programs at an amphitheater, guiding on a trail, or presenting outreach programs to schools or civic meetings. You could also be responding to guest needs at an information desk, answering questions on the phone, chatting with people on the museum floor, conducting demonstrations in an ecological exhibit at a zoo, or helping guests spot wildlife from the deck of a cruise boat.

Personal interpretation is one of the most powerful approaches to interpretation because the interpreter can continually adapt to each audience. If you are practicing personal interpretation, the opportunities for you to make emotional and intellectual connections are numerous, because you can learn about the guest and apply what you learn to enhance her or his experience. However, personal interpretive services are usually available for a limited amount of time each day and perform variably, depending upon the skill of the interpreter and how she or he feels at any given time. And personal interpretation is usually more expensive than nonpersonal approaches, when one considers the cost per visitor contact.

Nonpersonal interpretation includes brochures, exhibits, signs, audiovisual shows, and other things that do not require an actual person in attendance. Freeman Tilden believed that personal interpretation was always more powerful when done well, and he cautioned against using gadgetry that cannot be maintained properly. He did grant that nonpersonal approaches are all right if an interpreter is unavailable and that in certain circumstances nonpersonal media could be effective. Tilden even suggested that "a good result by device is better than a poor performance by an individual" (1957. *Interpreting Our Heritage*. Chapel Hill: University of North Carolina Press). But he was concerned that a poorly performing gadget actually lessens an experience to the extent that it would be better to have no interpretive services at all.

The decision to use personal or nonpersonal interpretive services is usually made by program managers and planners. Often, a combination of both is the best choice for a particular situation. Interpreters may find it helpful to develop nonpersonal interpretive items as aids to personal programs, such as interpretive brochures or wayside exhibits. It's important to note that the same interpretive principles discussed for personal interpretation also apply to nonpersonal media. If you are interested in learning more about nonpersonal interpretation, we recommend Sam Ham's *Environmental Interpretation* and the Interpreter's Handbook Series by Michael Gross and Ron Zimmerman as good beginning references.

Principles of Interpretation

Every profession has guidelines that help practitioners be more effective. Although Enos Mills introduced many ideas in *Adventures of a Nature Guide and Essays in Interpretation* (1920) that appear in more modern references, he did not organize those ideas as a set of specific principles. Freeman Tilden introduced that concept in his classic book *Interpreting Our Heritage* in 1957. In almost half a century of application by tens of thousands of interpreters, Tilden's six principles (paraphrased in the following paragraphs) have been found to be excellent rules of the trail and tour. Some examples in application of these principles follow.

Principle 1: Relate what is being displayed or described to something within the personality or experience of the visitor. How can you say things that help your audience feel some immediate connection to your subject? If showing a group of tourists a piece of baleen from a whale's mouth, you might ask, "How many of you have used a colander or strainer in your kitchen to strain peas or macaroni from a pan of water? A whale uses its baleen in a very similar way to strain krill from cold ocean waters." If most members of your audience have used a kitchen strainer, this example was a great choice. If they were children and had no kitchen experience, a different choice would be better for relating baleen to their experiences. In 2001 Mary Bonnell, a Certified Interpretive Trainer training docents at at Ocean Journey aquarium in Denver, Colorado, had children take a mouthful of Jello with nuts in it. By squeezing the Jello outward through their teeth, they trap the nut pieces in their mouths, demonstrating how baleen works in trapping krill while expelling water.

Principle 2: Information, as such, is not interpretation. All agree that information is essential to good interpretation but that it should not stop there. If you are a guide at a botanic garden and say, "This is a willow tree," you have been factual, but this statement alone is not likely to make a connection with the guest. Instead, you could say, "This is a willow tree, and Native Americans used the inner bark to

Why NAI Certifies Interpretive Guides

The Federal Interagency Council on Interpretation (FICI) began in 1986 as an informal gathering of federal chiefs of interpretation with Lisa Brochu as the first facilitator. With the creation of NAI in 1988, FICI was urged to formalize its meetings and now serves as a place for chiefs and managers of interpretive programs with federal agencies to share ideas and challenges on a regular basis. As NAI's executive director, I attend to provide liaison with NAI and the profession in general.

I was attending the quarterly FICI meeting in Washington, D.C., in April 1998. Each agency reported on the number of volunteer hours in interpretation generated among their varied parks, forests, and other sites. The total number of volunteer interpreters involved amounted to more than 275,000 individuals working for four different federal agencies. We discussed how organizations have begun to rely more and more on volunteers and docents for frontline communications. And we could each think of dozens of museums, aquaria, zoos, and nature centers that have fifty or more volunteer guides and interpreters. I was amazed to learn that the estimated fifteen thousand full-time interpreters in the United States are outnumbered eighteen to one by volunteers, docents, and seasonal guides or interpreters. Clearly the public often meets this group of guides more than they encounter the full-time people. Many of the latter are volunteer coordinators, interpretive trainers, and facilitators for these extensive volunteer and docent programs.

This information led the NAI Board and staff to discuss the potential benefits of training these seasonal, volunteer, and new-hire interpreters with no previous experience in the field. Although NAI began a certification program for experienced professionals in 1998, it had no category for certifying this important and rather substantial contingent of people practicing interpretation.

In May 2000, the Certified Interpretive Guide (CIG) category and course was added to the certification program. Its purpose is to provide training for new or seasonal interpreters without the experience or educational background to qualify for the other four professional certification categories. It is hoped that this CIG "basic training" for guides and interpreters will become the standard in the profession. If zoos, aquaria, historic sites, nature centers, museums, botanic gardens, cruise companies, tour companies, and parks all train toward the same basic standard, we have hopes that the overall quality of personal interpretive services will continue to improve. If we do our job well, we believe it will lead to the development of more paid positions as coordinators, trainers, and front-line interpreters, as well as better pay for all those in the profession.

—*T.M.*

Above: Walt Disney World interpreters at Animal Kingdom do personal interpretation for guests in a variety of settings, including this raptor program at Discovery Island. Photo by Tim Merriman. Left: Nonpersonal interpretation, such as this exhibit at the Hawaii Nature Center on Maui, provides an opportunity to tell the story when an interpreter is unavailable. Photo by Lisa Brochu.

make a medicine. Can anyone tell me what we take today for pain and fever that contains the same active ingredient?" Now you've made a connection for anyone in the audience who has ever treated pain or fever with aspirin. And you've used a question to engage your audience. You have gone beyond information to interpret the importance, or meaning, of a willow tree.

Principle 3: Interpretation is an art, which combines many arts. Any art is to some degree teachable. If you are a guide in a historic home, you might choose to dress in period costume and speak in the voice of a servant who worked in the home during an important time in the story of the historic site. Or you might relate a story that happened to the family who lived there that reveals more about their lives. Or perhaps you know a song from the period that expresses the feelings that the family might have experienced. These artistic approaches are more powerful in connecting with people than a purely narrative tour. Everyone is creative to varying degrees and can each enhance specific artistic skills. If you find it difficult to come up with creative ideas for interpreting your site, you can take seminars and training on using the arts in interpretation to make your presentations more effective.

Principle 4: The chief aim of interpretation is not instruction, but provocation. You take your tour group to the middle of a famous bridge in Concord, Massachusetts, and say, "Ralph Waldo Emerson wrote, 'Here once the embattled farmers stood, And fired the shot heard round the world, And America's War for Independence was begun.'" Or you could say, "The Revolutionary War began here with a battle between the British and American patriots on April 19, 1775." Which punches your internal buttons and makes you think? The first choice is unquestionably more thought-provoking for an audience learning about the beginning of the War for American Independence. Provocative efforts engage people and bring them into an interpretive experience. They also encourage the audience to investigate further on their own after the program is done.

Principle 5: Interpretation should aim to present a whole rather than a part, and must address itself to the whole person rather than any phase. You are leading a tour on a wetlands trail at Rocky Mountain National Park, Colorado, that traverses a beaver pond. You show the group a stump with obvious chew marks made by a beaver. You explain that a beaver did the gnawing. Your guests might be fascinated or they might yawn—a beaver, so what? Instead, you could tell the story of how small beaver ponds formed by the cutting and damming of small trees create vast aquatic ecosystems in the mountains used by dozens of animal species for food and habitat. You might relate the water cycle of a mountain system to the water system in the hometown of your guests and explain that the engineers (beavers) in the mountains play as vital a role as the hydrologists and engineers at your domestic water treatment plant. This second approach tells the bigger story behind a beaver-gnawed stump and relates it to people who drove to the mountains from their homes in the suburbs.

Principle 6: Interpretation addressed to children should not be a dilution of the presentation to adults, but should follow a fundamentally different approach. Imagine that you are a guide with groups at a zoo. Sometimes your group is all adults, and other times it is all children. When you show adults the aviary, you talk about the ecosystem and ask them to look at the beaks and feet of birds and think about what the birds might eat with those kinds of tools to acquire food—an intellectual exercise. With a children's group, you might ask the kids to demonstrate how birds walk and the sounds they make, and then have them try to guess why the varied walks and sounds help them survive. Playing games that engage an active imagination and allow acting things out is effective with youngsters. The same activity with a group of adults might fall flat. Learning styles change as people mature, and good guides and interpreters employ different strategies with people in different age groups.

The Power of Personal Style and Passion

In addition to his six principles, Tilden also said, "Le style, c'est l'homme." It is the person, the guide, the interpreter who makes something special happen. It is delivery with style and enthusiasm that works best. Each interpreter has to find her or his own special voice. Therein lies the art of interpretation, applying the scientific principles of interpretation to help audiences make emotional and intellectual connections with meanings inherent in the resources.

Tilden referred to love as "the priceless ingredient" in interpretation. He observed that the best interpreters are passionate about their subjects. Interpreters let their internal lights and loves illuminate what they share.

Larry Beck and Ted Cable updated Tilden's principles in *Interpretation for the 21st Century: Fifteen Guiding Principles for Interpreting Nature and Culture* (1997). They embraced Tilden's principles completely but then added nine more important ideas. And like Tilden's "priceless ingredient," Cable and Beck emphasized in the fifteenth principle that passion is important to success. More than likely, you work in this field because you are passionate about the resources and their importance. You want to employ that enthusiasm and energy in your programs, because it makes your interpretation more powerful and motivational.

Cable and Beck's updated principles bring to light many important points relevant to today's interpreters. Of special interest are numbers 8 and 12. Principle 8 suggests that technology can be a valuable tool; however, there is no reason to use gadgetry for its own sake. If the technology supports and enhances the program, then by all means, take advantage of it. But if it detracts from or overrides the message, pull the plug.

Principle 12 is increasingly important in an economy that often forces us to make difficult decisions about what we can and should provide the public. In Chapter 4, we'll discuss how your interpretive program can be used to support your organization's mission in measurable ways.

Cable and Beck's Fifteen Principles

1. To spark an interest, interpreters must relate the subject to the lives of the visitors.

2. The purpose of interpretation goes beyond providing information to reveal deeper meaning and truth.

3. The interpretive presentation—as a work of art—should be designed as a story that informs, entertains, and enlightens.

4. The purpose of the interpretive story is to inspire and to provoke people to broaden their horizons.

5. Interpretation should present a complete theme or thesis and address the whole person.

6. Interpretation for children, teenagers, and seniors—when these comprise uniform groups—should follow fundamentally different approaches.

7. Every place has a history. Interpreters can bring the past alive to make the present more enjoyable and the future more meaningful.

8. High technology can reveal the world in exciting new ways. However, incorporating this technology into the interpretive program must be done with foresight and care.

9. Interpreters must concern themselves with the quantity and quality (selection and accuracy) of information presented. Focused, well-researched interpretation will be more powerful than a longer discourse.

10. Before applying the arts in interpretation, the interpreter must be familiar with basic communication techniques. Quality interpretation depends on the interpreter's knowledge and skills, which should be developed continually.

11. Interpretive writing should address what readers would like to know, with the authority of wisdom and the humility and care that comes with it.

12. The overall interpretive program must be capable of attracting support—financial, volunteer, political, administrative—whatever support is needed for the program to flourish.

13. Interpretation should instill in people the ability, and the desire, to sense the beauty in their surroundings—to provide spiritual uplift and to encourage resource preservation.

14. Interpreters can promote optimal experiences through intentional and thoughtful program and facility design.

15. Passion is the essential ingredient for powerful and effective interpretation—passion for the resource and for those people who come to be inspired by the same.

Audience members learn traditional dances during a program in Hawaii. Photo by Lisa Brochu.

Docents at Colorado's Ocean Journey in Denver give children a "hands-on" opportunity to learn more about turtles. Photo by Tim Merriman.

A Renaissance harpist in authentic costuming brings the art of the luthier, bard, and interpreter together to interpret the 1700s to visitors. Photo by Tim Merriman.

The Experience Economy Theory in Practice

In 1998, I was vacationing in the Kailua-Kona area on the "Big Island" of Hawaii. I had been invited by Rob Pacheco, owner of Hawaii Forest and Trails, to go on an interpretive hike to the north coast of the Big Island. I met Danny Almonte, their interpretive guide, at a local restaurant and rode the van up to the Waikoloa Hilton to pick up their clients for the day, a young couple from England and a young woman from Japan. Danny explained on the drive that he was born on Kauai and that he was proud to be a native Hawaiian. He shared many stories from Hawaiian folklore while driving. Our destination was the valley where a boy known as Kamehameha was taken at the age of ten to be hidden by friends. It was prophesied that a boy would be born to royalty in the islands and that this boy would unite all of them under one king. King Kamehameha did just that much later in life.

We climbed out of the van at a pasture with conveniently placed portable toilets to be given a needed restroom break before setting out on foot in the "valley of the spear poles." The beautiful hike past and even behind gushing waterfalls was memorable. The glimpses of island history were wonderful, with stories of the boy who would be king, the Chinese workers who hollowed aqueducts out of the volcanic rock, and the invasion of exotic plants into the unique ecosystems of the islands. Danny performed well as our guide, and we returned to the van in a few hours, tired and hungry—inspired by the story of the valley and Kamehameha.

By the van, Danny spread out a small table with island-made nut breads, fresh fruit, juices, and ice water. It was just right as a finish to the journey. Soft drinks and chips would not have ended the day with the same flavor or texture. He drove us back to our lodging and let us know that T-shirts were available if we wanted mementos of the experience.

People pay a fair but substantial price for this half-day hike, but the entire experience is worth what the tourist pays. Hawaii Forest and Trail takes its reputation seriously and so does not want to disappoint its guests. Guides balance content with time to reflect, and they take care of the basic needs of tourists for restroom breaks, food, and cool water. When you leave the experience they create, you want to remember it, and my photos from that day bring it back every time. And, of course, I bought the T-shirt because it serves to remind me of the experience.

This program certainly used all of the important traits of a well-designed experience. It makes emotional and intellectual connections between the audience and the incredible resources of the island. Our "basic needs" were met, so our knowledge and awareness grew as we hiked. We had an incredible experience, a "peak experience" for me, as noted psychologist Abraham Maslow might have described it. Successful tour companies know how to mix hospitality with interpretive storytelling. They use tangibles and intangibles to get to the universals. And while it's happening, you are not even aware of it. You are simply having the experience.

—*T.M.*

An Approach to Communication

In *Environmental Interpretation: A Practical Guide for People with Big Ideas and Small Budgets,* Sam Ham writes, "Interpretation is simply an approach to communication." Ham's communication process is based on four qualities that can be used as a recipe for success in almost every personal interpretation program:

- Interpretation is enjoyable.
- Interpretation is relevant.
- Interpretation is organized.
- Interpretation has a theme.

Interpretation Is Enjoyable

The people you meet as interpretive audiences are usually with you voluntarily. They are not obligated to pay attention when you speak or demonstrate something you think will be interesting. Indeed, they can simply leave if sufficiently bored. At a park, your program may be competing against a snooze in a hammock or a picnic. In a zoo, your audience may be choosing between your presentation and watching the animals enjoy a snack. On a cruise, your personal touch is being compared to the experience of enjoying the scenery in solitude. You must add value to the guest's experience, or you can reasonably expect to be tuned out or abandoned. That's not the worst of it. If you bore your guests, they might tell their friends, and so you lose future audiences as well.

Interpretation Is Relevant

Ham writes that relevance "has two qualities: it's meaningful and it's personal." He explains that meaningful refers to having "context" within your brain. The terminology is familiar. You can relate to what is being said and understand it. This is the same as "making intellectual connections" in the language of our preferred definition. You can help people make intellectual connections through the techniques you use. Ham refers to this as "bridging the familiar and the unfamiliar." By using examples, comparisons, and analogies, you can connect something that the guest already knows to something new that you are introducing. Specialized comparisons such as metaphors and similes are particularly useful in making these "intellectual connections."

Making your presentation more personal refers to making "emotional connections." Ham says interpreters must present to an audience "something they care about." Using personal pronouns such as "you" will make people feel more involved. Questions such as, "How many of you have ever....?" or "Can you remember when you last saw...?" are compelling ways to engage people. Statements that include others can also create connections, such as, "Those of us who love birds have learned that...." When you make emotional connections with your guests, you give the intellectual information more importance. They are more likely to remember facts when they care about the resource.

Interpretation Is Organized

Ham, in his book *Environmental Interpretation,* writes that "interpretation, at its best, does not require a lot of effort from the audience." Organizing the presentation into an introduction, a body, and a conclusion can make it easier for the audience to follow and understand. According to research by David Ausubel, an audience can follow a presentation better when they know where it is going (1960. "The Use of Advance Organizers in the Learning and Retention of Meaningful Verbal Material." *Journal of Educational Psychology* 51:267–272). Ham also cites George Miller (1956. "The Magical Number Seven, Plus or Minus Two: Some Limits on Our Capacity for Processing Information." *The Psychological Review*), who conducted research referred to as "the magical number seven, plus or minus two." The general idea coming from Miller's work is that an audience can carry away only a limited number of distinct ideas or messages. Just about everyone can grasp and remember five individual ideas. A few audience members will remember as many as nine. In nonformal settings, you really want everyone in your audience engaged in what is happening and carrying away your ideas or messages. Five is the greatest number of distinct ideas you can use with surety that all in your audience will be able to handle them.

Interpretation Is Thematic

Ham writes that "the theme is the main point or message a communicator is trying to convey about that topic." Ham attributes his personal introduction to thematic interpretation to William Lewis, author of *Interpreting for Park Visitors.* In the *Legacy* magazine interview of him in 2000, Lewis said, "When a person finishes talking to you, you should be able to sum up what that person has said in one sentence." Thematic interpretation is a way of making interpretation the most effective form of communication that can be used by you, as a guide or interpreter, in natural and cultural heritage communications.

NPS Interpretive Equation

The National Park Service has its own take on the process of interpretation. The NPS Interpretive Development Program curriculum's Module 101 combines all the elements of successful interpretation in an easy-to-remember equation that reminds interpreters to keep balance among the variables in their work:

Knowledge of audience + Knowledge of resource x Application of appropriate techniques = Interpretive opportunity

or

$(Ka + Kr) \times AT = IO$

The beauty of this approach lies in its simplicity. If you combine knowledge of your audience (*Ka*) with your knowledge of the resource (*Kr*) and apply appro-

Above: Hawaii Forest and Trail guide Danny Almonte tells a traditional Hawaiian story about Pele's curse to a Japanese tourist.

Left: Almonte shares stories of King Kamehameha's youth on the trail at Pololu Valley. Photos by Tim Merriman.

priate techniques (*AT*), you can provide an interpretive opportunity (*IO*). It's important to note that the equation works only if the knowledge base and the presentation techniques are balanced. Too much information can make for an ineffective presentation, while too many gimmicks and gadgets in presentation style can overpower the message.

Another important point in this approach is that you can provide "interpretive opportunities," but you cannot guarantee that interpretation or the revelation of meaning will actually take place. Achieving that revelation is an internal process for the visitor. At best, you can provide the setting and appropriate communication techniques to help it occur.

The NPS also recommends a thematic approach to interpretation but goes one step beyond the previously mentioned thematic concepts. NPS trainers suggest that the best themes are those that connect tangible items to intangible ideas. This approach meshes nicely with their definition of interpretation, since many visitors come to a site initially interested in the "things" associated with the site, which may include the great views or unusual artifacts. By providing interpretive opportunities, the NPS hopes to facilitate connections to the meanings or the intangible ideas behind the "things" for a more complete visitor experience.

Providing Complete Experiences

In the July/August 1998 issue of the *Harvard Business Review,* authors Joseph Pine II and James H. Gilmore described the emerging economy in the United States as the "experience economy." Their metaphor for the changing economies was built around the birthday cake. In the agriculture economy, your mother baked a cake from scratch with local ingredients. In the manufacturing economy, Mom bought a cake mix, added some ingredients, and baked you a cake. Along came the service economy, and she picked up the entire cake, including decorations, at the local supermarket. In today's experience economy, she takes you and your buddies to Chuck E. Cheese or the Discovery Zone, and you get the cake, games, prizes, and a meal—an entire experience.

According to Pine and Gilmore, experience economy businesses have five basic elements. They all attempt to (a) harmonize impressions with positive cues, (b) eliminate negative cues, (c) engage all five senses, (d) theme the experience, and (e) mix in memorabilia (souvenirs).

The application of this theory to interpretation is obvious. Most good interpretive programs have employed some or all of these elements for a long time. As early as the 1970s, we were teaching interpreters that a good campfire program started with introductions, a song or two, a great slide presentation or demonstration, audience participation whenever possible, and closure with music or quotes followed by thematic food. Think in terms of crafting complete guest experiences as a guide or interpreter, and you will begin to create more lasting emotional connections for your guests.

NAI's Interpretive Approach

Given all the great communicators and researchers who have contributed to the body of knowledge about the process of interpretation, NAI has elected to combine what seem to be the most effective methods into its training materials. So the NAI interpretive approach is not simply one approach but a synthesis of many philosophies which all contribute to the larger picture of helping facilitate connections for the visitor while also helping your employer achieve goals and objectives. You, as the interpreter, are the link between the resource, the visitor, and the manager of the resource.

In the next two chapters, we'll look more closely at many of the individual elements we've already discussed in general terms to get a better sense of how to incorporate the most appropriate components of these approaches into your presentations.

Recommended Reading

Beck, Larry, and Ted Cable. 1998. *Interpretation for the 21st Century.* Champaign, IL: Sagamore Publishing.

Ham, Sam. 1992. *Environmental Interpretation.* Golden, CO: North American Press.

Tilden, Freeman. 1957. *Interpreting Our Heritage.* Chapel Hill: University of North Carolina Press.

If you've read the previous three chapters, you're probably feeling like you've got a pretty good handle on what interpretation is all about. Now comes the tricky part—figuring out how to apply all that background to an actual program. Let's look at some of the components we've described to see how you can relate them to the reality of the presentations you'll be giving.

Understanding Your Audience

Have you ever made a phone call and heard what you thought was a familiar voice answer? You probably talked to the person in a fairly casual way before realizing it wasn't who you thought. And what you said no doubt made no sense to them because you started into a story you thought they already knew something about. An interpretive audience is sort of like that phone call. If we assume we know who's listening to us or launch into a story that makes perfect sense to us but starts at a level of knowledge unfamiliar to the audience, we may completely misread their interest level and prior knowledge. When that happens, we fail at communication. In essence, we have to "hang up" and start over.

When asked who attends your programs, it is tempting to say, "the average visitor." In fact, there is no such animal. Every audience member is unique, and each group of unique individuals has its own attributes. Audiences can be described in a variety of ways—by age, gender, ethnicity, income levels, or family status. Families with young children, "empty nesters," and seniors are some of the more common demographic generalizations about audience subgroups. But you should also be interested in knowing where they are from—cities, towns, farms, near or far—and why they have chosen to come to your program.

There are many ways to learn more about our

4

PROGRAM

PREPARATION

interpretive audiences. Marketing studies can tell us a lot, but they can be expensive to conduct. And studies that use questionnaires or interviews are often skewed by the questions that are asked and the way they are asked. Still, market surveys are important sources of information because they give us an overall sense of what people want in their interpretive experiences.

Research by cruise companies has shown that their customers are mostly forty or older, experienced travelers, well educated, fairly affluent, and interested in learning while traveling. That kind of information provides a starting point. Walking the parking lot at a park, zoo, aquarium, or museum will give you a general idea of the out-of-state attendance just by glancing at license plates. Reading comment cards or the sign-in book and checking with the front desk to learn the top five questions that people ask can also tell you a lot about your audiences and their interests. Remember, though, that these methods are not scientific and simply provide some interesting insights.

When the audience is in front of you, you have a golden opportunity to learn from your guests: How many of you have been here before? How many have been here more than three times? Who has seen the new panda habitat? Who is from here in town? These are just a few of the many questions you might ask. Listening for the answers is important. As you gain experience, you will be able to incorporate references that apply to your unique audience members on the spur of the moment.

In some settings, you may need to find out who speaks your language. Many guides with ecotour businesses, cruise companies, and some parks have audiences made up substantially of people who speak other languages. Guides and interpreters who speak two or more languages are critical in these settings. Perhaps more important than understanding multiple languages, they must also have some fundamental understanding of other cultures. What do these people find interesting? What are their desires for recreational activities? How do they differ from the primary audience we encounter as guides or interpreters? What motivates them? Might they be offended by anything in our presentations?

Maslow's Hierarchy: What People Need

Noted psychologist Abraham Maslow presented a theory that explains the motivations and needs of people. In his book *Motivation and Personality* (1954. New York: Harper & Row Publishers, Inc.), Maslow separated these needs into two groups: basic needs and growth needs. Basic needs are those that apply to almost every animal species, relating to physiological, safety, and security needs. We all need air, food, water, sleep, and sex, according to Maslow, and we want to feel safe and secure while we're involved in getting those things. If basic needs are not being met, we are not likely to be interested in growth needs, something many researchers feel are uniquely human. Growth needs include love and belonging, self-esteem, and self-actualization. Self-actualization is described as "developing one consistent yet flexible lifestyle to become that self which one truly is."

Take Your Cue from What's in Front of You

I was making reservations for an interpretive boat tour by telephone. In my native Texan twang, I asked about the costs and times for the tour and was told that the cost of the tour was $50 if I went at 1 p.m., but only $35 if I went at 9 a.m. Naturally I opted for the 9 a.m. tour. I hung up the phone, happy with my savings. Then it occurred to me that there must be a reason why the nine o'clock tour was less expensive. Suddenly suspicious, I called back and asked about the difference in price. It seems the nine o'clock tour was offered in Japanese only.

I'm not sure why the Japanese tour merited a less expensive fare, but more to the point, I was amazed that the reservations clerk had failed to mention that critical piece of information when I was clearly an English speaker. Not speaking a word of Japanese, I would not have been a happy camper if I had shown up for the Japanese-only version of the tour.

There is much to be learned by listening and looking at the audience in front of you, if you simply take the time and pay attention. And having learned all you can, you can use that information to create meaningful experiences for your guests.

—L.B.

Maslow's Hierarchy of Needs, as the theory is called, is important to guides and interpreters because interpreters are usually trying to help people reach "self-actualization," so that they have what Maslow called a "peak experience," if possible. The goal is to help them make emotional connections with the resource that will last a lifetime and bring them back for similar experiences. If you lead a tour and forget to remind guests to take a restroom break before leaving on a long hike, or if you ignore building thunderclouds and lead them into a rainstorm experience, you may have problems getting your message across. Guests cannot appreciate your stimulating interpretation when they are wishing they had a restroom nearby or wondering if they will arrive safely back where they started.

When you take the time to help people meet their basic needs, you open up the opportunity for them to fully enjoy a tour, hike, or interpretive experience. A whale breaching near your tour boat may be the "peak experience" of a lifetime for a family who saved for years to take the tour, but if they are crouched on the gunwhales being sick because they did not prepare for rough seas, the whale experience will go unrealized. They remember the day only for its misery.

If you think of the hierarchy of needs as a staircase that advances from basic needs through esteem, knowledge, and understanding to self-actualization, you should be aware that most guests won't climb the entire staircase each tour. They need to explore and develop a greater understanding at their own speed. When they can relax about concerns for their own safety, they can stop and smell the flowers. You simply need to be aware of this process and plan your programs to satisfy basic needs easily so that your guests have a chance to realize growth needs.

Above: A tour guide at the Summer Palace in Beijing, China, gathers his yellow-capped group together to deliver his message. Left: This guide at Longwood Gardens in Philadelphia, Pennsylvania, holds a training manual containing relevant information about the resources of the botanical gardens. Photos by Tim Merriman.

What People Want

It's usually easy to determine what your audiences need. With the help of Maslow's Hierarchy and your own knowledge, you can identify ways in which you can address those needs within the time, space, and monetary boundaries of your programs. Not so easy to determine is what your audience wants. Yet understanding this crucial component may make the difference in whether your audience leaves fulfilled or disappointed.

To help you understand what audiences want, you can take a look at some basic marketing concepts of supply and demand. You supply a program, but the visitor holds the key to the demand for that program. Demand is defined as the desire and the ability to pay for what is being supplied. Desire seems logical enough. If people are interested, they will come. Ability to pay is a little harder to understand. People pay not only with dollars but also with their time. In other words, they must be interested enough to be willing to give up their precious leisure hours to participate in your program.

There are two ways to look at that information. One is to say that you're going to talk about the resource that's in front of you in a way that interests the interpreter and hope that your enthusiasm for the resource is enough to catch and hold the visitor's interest as well. This approach is generally considered a "resource-driven program." Or you can listen to what people ask for (through questions at the visitor center or tour registration office, or through questions and comments at other programs) and begin to craft your programs in such a way that they deliver the stories that the audience is truly interested in, rather than what personally interests you. This approach is called a "market-driven program."

Sometimes the best approach is a combination of program-driven and market-driven. Clearly, if you're interpreting a spectacular feature such as the Grand Canyon, you will be delivering a program about that particular resource (rather than showing slides about your recent trip to see polar bears, for instance); however, if you take the time to find out what aspect of the Grand Canyon your visitors are curious about, you may be able to connect with them more completely. Responding to your market (audience) does not mean that you ignore the resource at hand in order to satisfy your audience interests.

Developing Your Message

Deciding what to talk about depends on three things: the resource at hand, the interests of the audience, and the desires of management. Notice that your personal preference is not part of the equation. Although it's always fun to focus on the things in which you have a personal interest, your job is not to satisfy yourself. Consequently it's likely that you'll need to research your topic to broaden your knowledge base sufficiently to support a program. If your personal interests overlap with the needs of the situation, it's a bonus because your natural enthusiasm for what you are doing will strengthen your delivery.

Researching the Resource

A good research plan will help you learn more about your topic so you can develop an appropriate theme and support that theme with solid information. Start by identifying your topic, then listing possible sources for images, ideas, or supporting facts. Add phone numbers or addresses for contacting the sources, specify the dates by which you need the information, and then check the items off as you get them done. Develop a filing system that will help you keep track of your notes. Get in the habit of adding to a "bright ideas" page that you can keep near your desk when you hear of a possible new source of information or come up with a great way to communicate something to an audience.

Think about using both primary and secondary sources as you research the resource. Primary sources supply firsthand information and are usually more reliable than secondary sources. But gathering information from primary sources may consume more time than you have on hand. Some ways to tap into primary sources might include interviews, original photography or videography, research studies you conduct, or direct observations. Secondary sources are certainly easier to obtain. Check your library for books, visit the Internet, examine official records and archives, find a photography service bureau, or investigate similar sites.

Whether you rely most heavily on primary or secondary sources, try to incorporate a variety of information sources into your research plan, including, at the very least, books, videotapes, web sites, and personal interviews and observations. Start keeping a journal to record interesting information, quotations, or perspectives from others. As your journal pages are filled, move them to a filing system or notebook so they stay easily at hand and can be shared with co-workers. Don't forget to record the name, date, and location of the source so you can provide proper attribution if you use the material.

If you use somebody else's ideas, words, or pictures in any form of presentation, you should acknowledge the original source, if known. You can do this by adding footnotes to written material, attributing the source as you speak, indicating the source after a direct quote, or showing a list of source material following your program (like rolling the credits after a movie).

As you gather information, be aware of any bias on the part of the information source. Remember that you are ethically bound to present a balanced view of your subject matter so your audience members can form their own opinions. There is no doubt that interpretation is a persuasive form of communication, but there is a fine line between persuasion and propaganda. Using balanced sources can help you distinguish between the two, allowing you to make your point while still respecting the visitor's right to decide how they want to process the information you present.

Look beyond simple facts for interesting tidbits and stories that might help people understand and relate to the material. Remember that people love a good story, unusual facts, inspirational thoughts, and things that evoke emotional or physiological responses. As you write what you've researched, always be thinking how you might make intellectual and emotional connections between the material you've collected and your audience. No matter how many facts you collect, your audience will still view the subject of your presentation through their own experiential filters. You can use that knowledge to your advantage as you develop your message, by connecting tangible items to intangible ideas.

Connecting Tangibles to Intangibles
Imagine that you have a goose feather with a long white blade. You pass it among a group of people on your tour and you ask each one to give just one word to describe the feather. They say, "smooth, white, gossamer, silky, delicate," and you agree that all of these words are good descriptors. You then explain that it is a quill feather that was cut on its tip, dipped in ink, and used to sign the U.S. Declaration of Independence. You again ask each person to give a word of description. Now they say, "freedom, history, patriotism, powerful, lasting." Knowing the story behind the feather allows people to find the meanings behind a seemingly simple artifact—what was just a pretty white feather suddenly becomes an important part of their cultural heritage.

Trainer David Larsen, citing Module 101 of the NPS curriculum, often says, "All good interpretation involves connecting a tangible to an intangible." Larsen demonstrates this concept very ably in classes at the NPS Mather Training Center and the USFWS National Conservation Training Center, where he instructs. He shows interpreters how a good presentation moves back and forth from the story of the place, artifacts, people, or things, to ideas, concepts, hidden meanings, stories, and the "big picture." The latter are the intangibles. If you were to chart the progress of his presentation, you would find that there are not necessarily symmetrical stairsteps where a tangible is explained and then connected to an intangible idea. You may spend more time on the tangible early in the talk, while demonstrating or showing the tangible items. Then, as you talk about the intangibles, you spend time taking the audience into their hearts to make emotional connections with the intellectual ideas introduced earlier. The movement back and forth between tangibles and intangibles is the shuttle that weaves the fabric of the story.

If you led a group down a trail, explaining that this was part of the actual path of the Cherokee Trail of Tears, you might show how compacted the ground is, how steep the hills are. You could talk about the sixteen thousand people in the forced march, the quantity of possessions they carried, and the distance they would walk in a day. These are all tangibles and simply give an intellectual picture of the Trail of Tears.

You might then ask the audience to imagine leaving the home of their births to walk more than a thousand miles with only what they can easily carry. You could explain that they will make this move on foot with their children and grandparents, many of whom will walk barefoot over rocks and through streams in the dead of winter. You could explain that one of three will die along the way and ask them to imagine how it must feel to lose a loved one in a strange place and be denied the right to honor their dead. They cannot camp at night due to the prejudice of local people. The intangibles of family, moving households, death, and prejudice are likely to connect for anyone in the audience.

Interpretation weaves these threads of the tangible into the threads of the intangible. The fabric that results is a story that your audience can touch and feel. It becomes real because life is not just a litany of facts. It is a blend of facts, ideas, meanings, and universal feelings—tangibles and intangibles.

If you stay with simple facts or tangible things, your presentation will be flat, and the minds of your guests will likely wander. If you start with ethereal ideas and intangibles and give no tangible examples, guests will be unable to grasp what you're trying to say because the ideas are not grounded in reality for them. Moving back and forth from real things to bigger ideas is engaging. It keeps minds actively involved in the story.

Defining Universal Concepts

Larsen suggests that "universal concepts" are intangibles with a capital "I." In other words, they are the intangible ideas that are likely to appeal to everyone, regardless of their individual experiential filters. Family, death, and prejudice are universal concepts because virtually all humans have those in their life experience. Not all people move their households a thousand miles, but most modern Americans move a time or two in their lives, so the "move" is a universal as well. If you continually bring the stories you share from the tangible artifacts, places, and circumstances to the intangible and universal ideas, you are likely to connect with any audience. A few of the many universals you can use in your presentations are family, love, friendship, joy, beauty, tragedy, pain, death, change, work, play, celebration, care, stewardship, freedom, pleasure.

If you showed guests a flight of Canada geese, you could talk about the speed at which geese fly, the migration route they follow, and their unerring navigation ability. Though interesting facts, you might connect more quickly with a guest by talking about the small groups of geese being family units—mom, dad, and five young of the year. Canada geese mate for life and travel in larger flocks that are much like a flying village. They all live together on the breeding grounds and then travel together while migrating, spending the winter together in the south. These facts about geese connect to universals such as family, village, and mating for life, which are more likely to mean something to people from any culture or background.

You cannot know enough personal information about the interests of each guest to make everything you say relevant to everyone's experience. Using universals gives you a better chance of connecting with all kinds of people. Choose media that illustrate your presentation well and you improve your chances of connecting even more. Photos tell a story that almost everyone will understand. Word pictures are wonderful and can be moving, but multicultural audiences who may not speak English as a first language will have more difficulty with a good verbal program than with a good visual program. It is common for an interpreter to use

THE MUFFLED DRUM'S SAD ROLL HAS BEAT
THE SOLDIER'S LAST TATTOO.
NO MORE ON LIFE'S PARADE SHALL MEET
THAT BRAVE AND FALLEN FEW.

Top: A native Hawaiian horseback guide makes the trail experience more memorable by sharing stories handed down within her own culture. Photo by Lisa Brochu. Immediately above: The gravestones of soldiers who died at the Battle of the Little Bighorn and unmarked graves of Native Americans evoke universal concepts, such as death, loyalty, conflict, and prejudice, that help interpret the events at this important site. Photo by Tim Merriman.

both verbal and visual media, but it's important to remember that the visual media are easier for most guests to understand. Demonstrations are even more powerful because they involve the audience personally in an experience with the resource. When you pull audience members into the demonstration to participate, it engages those people and the other visitors who watch and enjoy the interaction.

Stating a Theme

Through his application of social and psychological theory, Ham has defined the approach to writing themes now used by most guides and interpreters. Simply put, Ham's philosophy is that "people remember themes, they forget facts." According to Ham, themes should:

- Be stated as short, simple, complete sentences
- Contain only one idea
- Reveal the overall purpose of the presentation
- Be specific
- Be interestingly worded (if possible, use active verbs)

Themes are messages or ideas we want to transmit. If you have no message, why are you doing the presentation? Ham points out that a theme should answer the "So what?" question so that your program has a point and is worthy of taking the audience's time. It's your obligation to develop a message that makes sense and that supports the mission of the organization. NPS trainer David Larsen suggests that a well-written theme should also connect a tangible item with an intangible idea, laying the groundwork for including those critical components in the program.

Ham writes about research by P.W. Thorndyke [1977. "Cognitive Structures in Comprehension and Memory of Narrative Discourse." *Cognitive Psychology* 9(1):77–110] that tested the power of themes in various placements within a presentation. Stating the theme near the beginning of a program launches the presentation in a direction that will make sense to the audience and lead them through the subthemes toward the conclusion. Reinforcing the theme in the conclusion has also been shown to be effective for bringing the talk full circle and providing closure.

In *Environmental Interpretation,* Ham recommends a three-step process to developing a theme.

Step 1. Select a general topic and use it to complete the following sentence: "Generally, my presentation is about…(the Cherokee Trail of Tears)

Step 2. State your topic in more specific terms and complete the following sentence: "Specifically, however, I want to tell my audience about… (what a tragic and sad journey it was for the Cherokee people)

Step 3. Now, express your theme by completing the following sentence: "After hearing my presentation, I want my audience to understand that… (the thousand-mile journey of the Cherokee Nation tells a story of tears and tragedy)

With the topic of the "Cherokee Trail of Tears," you can use the process to develop a theme of "The thousand-mile journey of the Cherokee Nation tells a story of tears and tragedy." Themes get you started and hint at the central purpose of the presentation. Like the marquee of a theater, a theme tantalizes and invites you into the experience. Ham's three-step process makes it easy for you to begin writing themes.

Five or Fewer Subthemes

A good presentation has not only a theme (main idea or message) but also has up to five subthemes (supporting ideas or message elements). Each subtheme should carry the same basic characteristics of a theme. Research by George Miller (1956. "The Magical Number Seven, Plus or Minus Two: Some Limits on Our Capacity for Processing Information." *The Psychological Review*) indicates that most humans can easily carry away five main ideas from any presentation, whether it be oral, written, or visual. Some people tested can retain more than that, but virtually everyone in the audience can leave with five or fewer ideas. If you have more than five subthemes, most will not be retained by your audience, and you may find that they leave with a different sense of your message or overall theme than you intended.

Examples

Theme: Toads lead a double life that may amaze you.

Subthemes:
1. Toads are the dryland "frogs" that love your garden bugs.
2. In spring the guys dive in the closest puddle to serenade the ladies.
3. Their noisy mating launches hundreds of hungry plant-eating tadpoles.
4. By fall the tadpoles grow legs, leave the puddle, and crave a bug diet.
5. By the next spring, these dryland "frogs" are hunting a puddle again.

Theme: The thousand-mile journey of the Cherokee Nation tells a story of tears and tragedy.

Subthemes:
1. From 1838 to 1839, more than fifteen thousand Cherokee people walked a thousand miles to a new home not of their choosing.
2. Cold, disease, and a lack of food claimed the lives of more than forty-six hundred Cherokee on the trek and eight hundred more in the first year in Oklahoma.
3. The Cherokee people remember the tragic march as the time their people cried; thus, the lasting name of the path became the Trail of Tears.

Subthemes help you sequence the supporting ideas in your presentation so that they make sense to the audience. Think about telling a simple joke. If you deliver the joke's key points out of sequence, the joke falls flat by the time you get to the punch line, and your audience is simply confused rather than amused. The

Left: This uniformed guide at Masaya Volcano National Park near Masaya, Nicaragua, tells the geological stories of the area while serving the mission of the organization. Photo by Tim Merriman.

same principle can be applied to your interpretive program. Use the subthemes to put your key points in a logical order that carries your audience through a progression of thought. By the time you restate your theme at the end of the program, they'll be right with you—they'll "get it" and be more likely to remember the message you've delivered.

Interpretation Has a Purpose

Most businesses and organizations have a stated mission. That mission statement can make the selection of your theme and subthemes relatively easy. If your mission is "to develop awareness among our guests of the significance of the ocean's resources," then you already have a starting point.

If you don't have a stated mission, ask your site manager or the business owner, "What is our purpose? or "Why do we exist?" Any for-profit business could say "to make money," but most have some broader purpose that gets at the motivations behind creating the business: "create quality family recreation" or "preserve and protect cultural resources of Louisiana," or "help people understand the fragile ecology of...."

A government agency usually has a published mission that states its purpose. This mission can often be found in the site's enabling legislation. Ideally it should be short and memorable—one simple sentence. Some organizations are inclined to write elaborate mission statements that cannot be easily remembered, but how do

A Tangible/Intangible Connection

In the fall of 1978, I was on a field trip with NAI to visit Tumacacori Mission National Monument, south of Tucson. A crowd of us were following the interpreter through the mission's exhibit area. For me there were too many people, too much distraction, text-intensive exhibits, and the appeal of the unique outdoors—the Sonoran Desert.

I left the tour and wandered out the back door onto the grounds of the area. A woman in colorful dress was working by an horno, a clay beehive oven used for baking bread in the U.S. Southwest. I walked over to see what she was doing. She smiled and handed me a ball of yellow dough. I asked if she spoke English, and she shook her head, so I switched to Spanish. She smiled again but apparently didn't speak Spanish either or at least not the Spanish I was using. She quickly patted out another ball of dough into a smooth, round tortilla and cooked it on the griddle over an open fire. I caught the idea and tried my hand with the ball of dough. The result was a ragged, amoeba-like tortilla that fell apart during the cooking process. She handed me her nice, neat tortilla when it was cooked, splashed salsa on it, and invited me to eat it, using her best pantomime. I enjoyed the fresh tortilla very much, the first one of its kind in my life. Her demonstration of native cooking was memorable. I still remember the entire experience and cherish it. I met this Tohono O'odham woman and conversed without words. She offered me food, always a touching human experience. I developed a sense of native food being fresh and easy, based on corn grown locally.

This brief impromptu program was virtually devoid of facts, but learning occurred. I enjoyed the food, the exchange with a native person, the glimpse of the origin of southwestern cuisine, and the reminder that natives were very much a part of the Spanish mission story. The experience left me wanting to know more about the mission, the area, the origins of southwestern cuisine, and the Tohono O'odham people. Good interpretive programs have these effects. Sharing food is a universal that may not be permitted in every program situation, but it is powerful when used well. When we share food, we share a special part of our cultural story, and it connects with smell, taste, touch, and visual pleasure. Even the sounds of the crackling fire and smoky breeze were present. With that multisensory approach to a universal concept, we can inspire with more than words.

—T.M.

you continually work toward the mission if you cannot remember it? If your agency or organization's mission is too long to remember, try to summarize it in a few words so it's easier to recall and repeat.

Goals are usually statements of long-range vision that support the mission of the organization. Ideally your organization has already determined goals during a strategic-planning session and you can just ask what they are. If they don't exist, you need to think about and talk about what goals you and your fellow guides and interpreters will pursue. Be realistic as you think about what interpretation can accomplish for your organization.

Remember the classic book by L. Frank Baum, *The Wizard of Oz?* If your name is Dorothy and you hail from Kansas, your goal might be to find true happiness. So what will help you achieve your goal? To find true happiness, you need to find the way home. Can you do that by taking a helicopter or a yellow brick road? Objectives help define ways in which you can achieve your goal. Following the yellow brick road is the beginning of an objective. It's a strategy, but as stated it's not a measurable strategy.

Many organizations and agencies now mandate that their employees use "outcomes-based management." Outcomes are measurable and reflect results, not process. Dorothy can say she will follow the yellow brick road. You could look at her progress and see if she does indeed follow that road. But she could follow it forever and it may never get her to Oz, where she will find the key to returning home. How will you know the objective is achieved? You need to define both the type and the extent of the outcome. If she says she will follow the yellow brick road to the city-limits sign of Oz, you have a destination with a milepost—an indicator that tells you the objective has been achieved. You could get more specific still and say that once she reaches Oz, she will find two ways to get home. But since you may not be as interested in Oz as Dorothy, let's apply goals and objectives to a park, an aquarium, a historic site, a cruise, or a nature center by looking at some examples.

Goal: Encourage the public to protect and conserve our cultural resources.
Objective: After tourists go through our interpretive program, incidents of vandalism in our historic sites this year will be reduced by 10 percent.

Goal: Facilitate a positive wildlife experience for guests on a cruise.
Objective: Eighty percent of guests will report seeing and will correctly identify at least three common wildlife species after they spend at least an hour with our naturalist.

Goal: Provide a safe experience for guests and wildlife in the park.
Objective: After visitors view our auto-tour interpretive signs, 15 percent fewer animal road kills will be found on park roads. Human accidents with wildlife will decline by 20 percent by the year's end.

Goal: We will provide a clean and natural environment at the nature center for guests.
Objective: After three months of offering our "Litter Be Gone" program, litter found on nature center grounds will be reduced by two cubic yards per month.

If you design interpretive programs around measurable objectives with well-defined mileposts, it is easy to evaluate your own success or to explain it to the boss. However, you should show your planned programs and their objectives to your boss or supervisor while planning. If they feel your plans realistically reflect organizational mission, goals, and objectives, you are good to go. If they don't see the alignment, talk more about it and try to get their ideas for what will more thoroughly support the overall organization.

Growing Your Creativity

Stating goals, objectives, themes, and subthemes may seem so structured that it has the potential to squash the artistic aspects of your presentation. But paying attention to the structure of a program might actually have the opposite effect. Once you know the parameters within which your message is to be delivered, your muse can go wild with creative possibilities for the presentation itself.

Interpretation is one of those disciplines that requires a workout on both sides of the brain. So if your left brain was getting settled in with the structure part of the discussion in this chapter and your right brain's been snoozing, it's time to wake it up and put it to work.

An unknown author once identified these four types of creative people:

Comatose creator: This person believes that if you just wait long enough, an idea will come to you through some divine intervention. Of course, if you wait too long, it won't matter, because someone else will have your job.

Constipated creator: This person tries hard to be creative, believing that if you force it, the idea will come. Unfortunately, once the idea squeezes out of your subconscious, it might not be in any shape to address the issue at hand.

Common creator: This stereotype of creative people has a diva complex. This person tortures himself and everyone around by being temperamental, stubborn, and absentminded, all in an effort to prove that he is creative.

Creative creator: The true creative spirit knows that if you prepare, concentrate, incubate, and illuminate your ideas, you will be successful in your quest for innovative ideas.

Everyone can be creative, even though some people tend to allow their right brains to get a little lazy from time to time. After all, it's usually easier to follow a formula than to come up with something different or new. Nevertheless it is possible to cultivate your creative side. You simply have to exercise it, just like an unused muscle. It might strain a little at first, but with regular use, you'll find it gets easier to come up with great ideas for delivering your message. In the next two chapters, we'll discuss some ideas for presentation techniques that allow your creative side to shine.

Recommended Reading

Campbell, David P. 1985. *Take the Road to Creativity and Get Off Your Dead End.* Center for Creative Leadership.

De Bono, Edward. 1990. *Lateral Thinking.* New York: Putnam.

Ham, Sam. 1992. *Environmental Interpretation.* Chapters 2, 6, and 7. Golden, CO: North American Press.

Knudson, Douglas M., Ted T. Cable, and Larry Beck. 1995. *Interpretation of Cultural and Natural Resources.* Chapters 3 and 4. State College, PA: Venture Publishing, Inc.

Raudsepp, Eugene. 1977. *Creative Growth Games.* New York: Putnam.

Von Oech, Roger. 1998. *A Whack on the Side of the Head.* New York: Warner Books.

Keep It Organized

Remember sitting around a holiday table, listening to a relative launch into a story of days gone by? Maybe it was your great-aunt Myrtle, telling about your second cousin once removed who married the boy down the street—he was a nice boy, now what was his name, and they moved to Albertsville, or was it Petersburg, but they had a dog, dogs are so cute, have you seen one of those little wrinkled dogs that come from China, you know they drink a lot of tea in China, and some tea would sure be good about now....

You get the idea. The story began and wandered aimlessly for an excruciatingly interminable time. Were you spellbound, or did your attention wander? Most likely, you tuned out everything after the word *cousin* and then checked back in when you heard the word *tea,* recognizing it as an opportunity to escape into the kitchen. You've probably attended a few interpretive presentations that took the same perilous path. Though there may have been individual words or phrases that drew your interest, you quite naturally invoked the power of selective listening and likely came away feeling no richer for the experience.

In *Environmental Interpretation,* Sam Ham points out that good interpretation is organized. It has a beginning, a middle, and an end. When you organize your thoughts (unlike Great-Aunt Myrtle), you can convey a specific message in a way that keeps your audience engaged for the entire length of the presentation, thereby increasing the chances that they will remember the message long after the presentation is over. Think in terms of the beginning (introduction), the middle (body), and the end (conclusion) as you prepare your presentation. Each of these three pieces can be further broken down into specific elements. Learning the elements that make up the introduction, the body, and the conclusion will help you organize your thoughts and develop a presentation that flows smoothly from beginning to end.

Begin at the Beginning: Writing the Introduction
People like to know what's going to happen. Though most people enjoy or at least take the occasional surprise in stride, you generally feel more comfortable if you have a sense of where you're headed. Educational psychologist David Ausubel called this an "advance organizer," something that lets people know where the presentation is going.

The introduction to your presentation gives you an opportunity to accomplish several things: (a) introduce yourself and your organization, (b) take care of any announcements, (c) find out a little about your audience, (d) address the basic needs of your visitors (see Chapter 3 on Maslow's Hierarchy), and (e) set the stage for what's coming. That's a lot to accomplish in a short time, but the introduction can make or break your program in a few simple sentences. It's your chance to hook your audience's interest and build a common bond with them that will keep them interested. Without a strong introduction, your audience's attention is likely to wander, tuning in and out to key words or phrases during the presentation, making it impossible for them to remember your point.

A good introduction structures the experience to come, so your audience knows what to expect and what is expected of them. It sets them at ease, so they can invest themselves wholly in your program. Whether you are presenting an in-place program or leading a hike, try to include the following elements in your introductory statements:

Who you are and who you work for. Always identify yourself, using the name that you would like your audience members to use for you. Be sure to work in the name of your organization. Don't assume that your audience knows what agency is represented by the insignia on your uniform.

What is going to happen. Give a quick overview of the program. A simple summation ("Today's program includes a short hike" or "We'll be watching a few slides before looking at real reptiles") can help the audience decide whether the program is for them before you really get started.

Where you're going and where you'll end up. If you'll be leaving the vicinity, let the audience know before they go, especially if you will end at a different location. Generally it's a good idea to plan your presentation so that you end up at the starting point to accommodate transportation or gathering needs of the visitors (for instance, if some family members elect to stay behind).

How long it's going to take. An approximation of the time investment required may make a difference in the participation of some audience members. Let them know about how long you'll be keeping them at the amphitheater, how much time it usually takes to complete the hike, or how long you'll be at each stop along the way (for extended tours).

Take care of those basic needs. If your program is relatively long (over an hour or two), be sure to indicate the availability of restrooms, water, first aid, and other items that audience members might need.

What will be required of the visitors. It's important to establish at the outset whether there will be any physical demands made on the visitor. If you notice someone who has obvious health problems, is dressed inappropriately, or seems otherwise unable or unwilling to participate in the program, it is your responsibility to take her or him aside and offer an option for staying behind or leaving the vicinity of the program. Handle the situation tactfully, but be aware that you or your organization may be held liable if you do not do an adequate job of preparing people for what may be required of them.

When it's appropriate to ask questions. Depending on your presentation and your personal style, you may want to direct the audience to ask questions informally during the presentation or hold their questions until the end. Generally, keeping an informal and open style that welcomes questions at any time makes for a more enjoyable experience; however, you must be careful that overly exuberant questioners don't commandeer the program or constantly derail your train of thought.

Theme statement. The introduction is the first chance you have to make a point. Use it wisely and creatively, to grab the attention of your audience. You'll want to support the theme statement throughout the body and then restate it during the conclusion.

Remember that this is your opportunity to establish a bond with your audience, so be creative with your introduction. Try using an attention-getting statement related to your theme. After greeting and welcoming her audience, Maria-Elena Muriel, a freelance guide in Cabo San Lucas, Baja California, Mexico, started a program with the prediction that, by the time the program was over, "whenever you see a plastic bag, you'll think of sea turtles." The two items in this theme statement seemed unrelated, creating a sense of intrigue about what was in store. She went on with the program, explaining the relationship between the sea turtle's life cycle and how that cycle can be disrupted by ingestion of plastic bags floating in the ocean.

You might want to start by sharing a personal experience that relates to your theme or by asking audience members to share briefly one of theirs. The introduction also provides an opportunity to find out what your audience already knows or is interested in by asking questions of them (see "Questioning Strategies" in this chapter).

It's not critical that you follow the above format in your introduction as long as the applicable elements are included. Some elements may not always be appropriate for each type of presentation, and sometimes the elements may need to be rearranged to emphasize certain points or to create a special atmosphere.

Smooth Moves: Writing Transition Statements

Within the body of your program, you'll be presenting two to five subthemes or ideas that support your theme (see Chapter 4, "Developing Your Message"). Ideally these ideas will flow smoothly from your introduction, then lead the audience through the body of your program to its natural conclusion. Transition statements help keep the flow going from one idea to the next and keep your presentation from sounding like a recitation of unrelated facts.

As you plan your presentation, think about how you will transition from one thought to another. If, for example, you're leading a guided tour through a desert area, you could use one stop to point out the identifying features of a cactus and then ask participants to look for other plants with those features while you move to your next stop. When you reach the next stop, take a few minutes and let your audience tell you what they saw. Their observations can then lead into your discussion at that stop, which might be a comparison between cacti and nonsucculent plants.

Transition statements can also be used to link one program to another, encouraging further participation immediately following a presentation or at a later date. Think of watching a television program that offers previously seen scenes at the beginning or next week's previews at the end. These are transition pieces that help the viewer understand what's come before or what will come next. You can apply the same technique to programs that might work best in a series of related sessions.

As you gain experience as an interpreter, you will be able to incorporate comments or questions from the audience as transitions from one thought to the next, helping to personalize each program for that particular audience. Until then, get in the habit of thinking through your transitions as you prepare your presentation outline (see Chapter 7, "Writing a Program Outline").

Wrap It Up: Writing the Conclusion

The conclusion could be the most important part of your presentation. Since it comes last, it will leave the biggest impression in the minds and hearts of your visitors. A weak conclusion may leave your audience frustrated or unhappy. On the other hand, a strong conclusion can reinforce your message and leave your audience wanting more—more information about the topic, more involvement on a personal level, more contacts with your agency or company.

To make your conclusion as strong as possible, try to incorporate the following elements:

Summary of subthemes and theme. Use the conclusion as an opportunity to restate your theme. You may want to state it in a different way than you did in the introduction, but your audience should realize that they've come full circle, back to the original thought, at the end of the program. If you've done your job well, they will be having a different reaction than they did at the beginning. They will have discovered a new way of looking at things that will travel home with them.

U.S. Army Corps of Engineers ranger Duane Johnson begins a guided hike at Stanislaus River Parks in California with an introduction to the significance of the site. Photo by Lisa Brochu.

Docents at the Waikiki Aquarium use discovery activities and small sea creatures to complement their message about protection of tide pools. Photo by Lisa Brochu.

Suggestions for continuing activities related to the theme. If you are aware of additional programs or activities that relate to your theme, providing that information to your audience will be appreciated by those whose interest you have stimulated. Tracking their involvement in additional activities (such as participating in a beach cleanup or signing up for another tour) can also help you determine whether your program objectives have been met.

Provocation of further thought or action. As Freeman Tilden suggests in *Interpreting Our Heritage,* interpretation should be provocative. By asking thoughtful questions or offering opportunities for taking action, your conclusion can provoke audience members in a way that will encourage further discovery on their own. You might also provoke additional questions. Jim Covel of Monterey Bay Aquarium in Monterey, California, has said that his site's interpreters like their audience to leave with more questions than when they arrived. Good interpretation leaves the audience wanting to know more, curious about what they yet might learn.

Opportunity to seek further information from you or your organization. Let the audience know if, how long, and where you'll be available to answer further questions or if you have reference materials available that guests can use to research something related to your theme. If appropriate, you might want to prepare handouts that indicate sources of reference materials or additional activities. Save these handouts for the conclusion so that visitors don't have to keep up with them or get distracted by them during the presentation.

Awareness of the example you provide. Make your actions consistent with the message in your theme. If you helped your audience understand the dangers that plastic bags present for turtles, be sure you notice litter as you walk and pick up pieces yourself. You'll find your guests will do the same and they will get the other message—that you believe and practice what you say.

Promotion of a good feeling about the site, agency, or company. Leave your audience with a smile—on their faces and yours. It's the last image they'll carry in their memories. Coupled with the good experience they've had attending your presentation, it will seal their commitment to coming back or telling others about their visit in a positive light.

Questioning Strategies

People enjoy being made to feel welcome and important. One simple way to get them involved in and keep them engaged with your presentation is to ask their opinions. Instead of standing in front of the group and setting yourself up as an expert as you "present" information, ask the audience what they think. You may find yourself surprised by their answers. Often you will uncover an expert in the group who can offer different perspectives on your topic. Instead of shutting the unexpected experts down, draw them into the presentation as a resource and open yourself to learning from them. Do be careful not to allow such a person to dominate the program or intimidate other visitors.

Questions can be used as an icebreaker in your introduction, providing a quick audience analysis that can be drawn upon later in the program. For example, if you ask whether any of the audience members have ever been to your site before, you can get an immediate sense of whether you need to provide a little or a lot of basic information about the site or resource. Some of their answers might also give you clues that will help you make your presentation more relevant, as Sam Ham suggests in *Environmental Interpretation*.

You might want to ask audience members about their expectations during your introduction. If their expectations turn out to be quite different from your program content, you then have an option for quickly rethinking your program strategy or for providing structuring comments that will let your audience know what will actually be delivered, giving them the option for participation or not. Keep these introductory questions simple and few. As you gain experience, you'll find which questions work best with which groups.

Developing a questioning strategy for your presentations can help your audience process the information you'll be introducing. Since they'll be actively involved in the program through the question-and-answer process, they will be more likely to retain the message. Although questions can be asked of the audience at any time, a logical sequence in the types of questions that you ask can be used to "pull" the audience through the program, allowing them to interpret their own observations.

Begin early in the program with open questions. These questions have no right or wrong answers. They are used to give everyone an opportunity to participate regardless of their experience or knowledge level. An open question might ask the audience to make an observation, such as, "What do you see as you look at the hillside?" or "What do you remember about the first sunset you saw?" Everyone will see or remember something different. It's not necessary or even desirable to get a response from everyone in the group, but you should allow those who want to contribute an observation to do so.

Most groups will include two or three people who readily supply answers to your questions. Other individuals might be hesitant to respond at first but can be drawn out if you look at them as you ask the question. As you gain experience in questioning, you'll be able to discern who might be likely to respond and who would prefer to be left alone. In any case, don't rush to supply an answer to your own question. Give the audience time to think, allowing up to fifteen seconds before you jump in. Studies have shown that the longer you wait, the more in-depth the response you will receive.

As the program continues, you might want to focus the audience's attention. Do this by asking data-recall questions. With these questions, you're asking for specific numbers, lists, or other facts based on previous information you've given or the visitor's prior experiences or observations. Though you're asking for specific information, try not to be judgmental in your responses. For example, you might ask, "What are some things that are helping this log decay?" Clearly there are correct answers for this question; however, there is also room for interpretation on the part of the audience, and creative thinking should be encouraged.

Once the audience's attention has been focused, ask the audience to interpret the data by thinking about comparisons or relationships that might apply. You might ask, "How does the wood strength or texture of these two trees compare?" Again, there are correct answers, but there are still opportunities for unexpected answers.

Towards the end of your program, perhaps as part of your conclusion, ask the visitors to summarize or apply a principle you've discussed. These capstone or application questions help the audience see things from a new perspective. Their answers may also shed some light on whether you've accomplished your objective. An example of an application question might be, "Now that we've seen how fires affect the forest, how do you think this area would be different if it hadn't burned?"

Questions, used with some forethought in a sequenced strategy, can get and keep your audience's attention, allow them to participate in your program, and give you an understanding of the audience's perceptions. However, questions can also be overused and become a hindrance to the progression of the program. Learning appropriate response strategies can help keep you on track with your questions and the audience from taking over the program.

The way you respond to the people who answer questions you've asked sets the tone for your interpretive program. If you are welcoming and receptive to visitor comments, more discussion is generated and the likelihood of success is enhanced. The most appropriate response will be dictated by the individual situation and the personal style of the interpreter.

The ideal response is an accepting one. Passive acceptance is indicated by a smile or a simple nod of the head, suggesting that you've heard the response and are saying the answer is okay without any additional judgment or evaluation. Active acceptance offers an expression of understanding, letting the visitor know that you comprehend what he or she has said. If you aren't sure what the visitor is saying, you might respond with a request for clarification. Finally, you can offer data to support their response in a number of ways. You can provide an opportunity for them to discover additional information on their own through experimentation or directed observation. You can also invite other audience members to supply information or refer to other sources you've brought with you.

Many visitors enjoy the opportunity to investigate or research information on their own if you simply direct them to the proper reference material. Bringing a bird book along and allowing the audience to look up an unidentified bird is often more effective than simply naming the bird for them. The process of looking up the information gives you the opportunity to talk about characteristics of different bird families and may give the visitor exposure to a new resource. Practice responding appropriately until an "accepting" response becomes second nature. It's easy to say no, especially when you know there is a correct answer, but negative responses tend to shut people down and discourage further participation. Making a habit of issuing positive responses makes it easy to answer with an encouraging smile. You might respond to a wrong answer with, "Thank you. That's a logical answer and what many of us have heard or been taught. However, the best answer is a little more complicated. Are there other suggestions?" You don't want to leave a guest believing something you know to be incorrect, but your correction has to be appropriate and gentle.

No matter how inappropriate a visitor's answer might seem, avoid ridiculing their attempt. No one likes to be laughed at, although if you have excellent people skills, you might be able to turn a potentially embarrassing answer into an opportunity to laugh with someone. Just be careful and cognizant of the individual's feelings before you go too far with trying to make a joke of their answer.

Recommended Reading

Ham, Sam. 1992. *Environmental Interpretation.* Golden, CO: North American Press.

Knudson, Douglas M., Ted T. Cable, and Larry Beck. 1995. *Interpretation of Cultural and Natural Resources.* State College, PA: Venture Publishing, Inc.

Make It Enjoyable

In *Environmental Interpretation,* Sam Ham suggests that interpretation should be pleasurable or enjoyable. How enjoyable is it to watch someone stand stiffly in front of a group and speak uninterrupted for twenty to thirty minutes? While you may enjoy hearing the sound of your voice, it's quite likely that a significant portion of the audience does not share your enthusiasm.

People process information in different ways. Some people are verbal learners who need to read the material, while others are auditory learners who prefer to have someone tell them what they need to know. You can tell which you are by whether you read the instruction manual for something yourself or have someone read it to you while you carry out the instructions. Visual learners need to see the actual object or a graphic representation of it for comprehension. These people are good map readers, because they generally think in terms of symbols. Kinesthetic learners like to interact with things, get their hands dirty, and do something physical that helps them understand how things work. Most children are simply learning kinesthetically when they head into a pond and stuff frogs in their pockets.

You can use the differences in learning styles to help you create a program that will be enjoyable for everyone in your group, if you try to incorporate elements that will appeal to two or more of the learning styles. For example, a tour of an ice cream factory might begin with a short video presentation that appeals to the verbal, visual, and auditory learners. When the video is over, the group moves to an overlook from which they can view the ice cream making and packaging processes (visual). On the walls are signs with text and graphic representations of the process and recipes (verbal, visual). The view and signs are complemented by the tour guide who provides information about what's going on and answers questions (auditory). Finally, the tour ends with an opportunity to make and eat your own ice cream (kinesthetic). Certainly, a program where you participate (not to mention getting to eat the subject matter) is more enjoyable than simply watching slides or listening to an "expert."

As you gain experience with interpreting to a variety of individuals, you'll begin to discover what types of illustrative techniques work best with what topics and groups. Not every technique described here is appropriate for every situation, but we offer a few ideas you can incorporate as needed to make your presentations more enjoyable.

Performing Arts: Music, Puppets, Poetry, Dance

We are all blessed with different talents for communicating creatively. Don't be afraid to use your talent to connect with your audience. Though interpretation is more than entertainment, there's nothing wrong with delivering your message in an entertaining way. The key is to remember that there is a message to deliver, so that you (and your audience) don't get so carried away with the fun of it all that you forget the purpose of what you're doing. If you don't consider yourself talented in any sort of performing art or with the written word, don't despair. There are plenty of talented people from whom you can borrow. Recordings of music, quotes from noted writers, and even enlisting the help of someone who may be comfortable strumming a guitar, but not with delivery of the program, are all options for bringing these elements into your presentation.

Music is a universal language that appeals to almost everyone. Even if you can't understand all the words, you can usually tell if the music is upbeat and positive (if you're using it to tell the story of bald eagle recovery, for example) or sad and foreboding (if you're using it to describe the pollution of a river). Music sets a mood. Often a word or phrase set to music will stick in your head for hours, days, or a lifetime. If you've been to a Disney theme park, just think of the song "It's a Small World" and you'll be hearing it in your head for the next five days, guaranteed. And it will come back every time someone mentions the phrase. Annoying as it may be, it's the stated theme of an amusement park attraction that sticks with you simply because it's been set to music.

Music allows and encourages audience participation. From simple sing-alongs of familiar tunes around the campfire ("This Land Is Your Land") to original compositions that focus on local issues (Bill Oliver's "Barton Springs Eternal" performed in Austin, Texas), songs that have easily learned repetitive phrases or hand motions can go a long way toward helping your audience remember your point, and have fun while doing it.

Right in step with the potential of music comes the possibility of adding dance steps. Dance can be performed for the audience or with the audience, depending on the individual situation and the willingness of audience members to participate. Whether you're interpreting the culture surrounding an antebellum home or the

Above: Dancers from the Marquesa Islands at the Polynesian Cultural Center on Oahu demonstrate the appeal of cultural interpretation using the arts with native dancers, full costumes, authentic music, and a unique outdoor setting. Photo by Lisa Brochu.

Left: A ladybug greets guests at Walt Disney World's Animal Kingdom to create excitement for children arriving at the popular theme park. Photo by Tim Merriman.

Low Key Also Strikes a Chord

Many times interpreters think making interpretation enjoyable means bouncing around the stage in full costume or being bubbly and vivacious. But sometimes a slower, more thoughtful approach is just as, if not more, enjoyable. One of my most memorable interpretive tours was taken on horseback in Hawaii. Given that the tour group consisted of only two people and the guide, I had the opportunity to specify that I preferred to have a quiet ride. The guide, a native Hawaiian who'd only been off the island once in her lifetime, complied with my request, simply answering the questions that I had along the way. But the way she answered them was something special.

If I asked the name of a plant, she not only told me its English name but also its Hawaiian name, and then a little story about it. Some of the stories were humorous, some were tragic, some had to do with the biological inter-relationships of the island, and some were made up on the spot, I'm sure. I was treated to a raft of Hawaiian culture in that hour and a half, quietly delivered in a conversational fashion. Whether she intended to or not, she managed to convey a thematic thread throughout her answers that I will never forget.

The experience led me to purchase a half dozen books on Hawaiian folklore and to recommend the hotel and its horseback ride to at least a half dozen people within the following week. Was it flashy and "entertaining?" Not a bit. Was it enjoyable? You bet. On reflection, it even seemed organized, thematic, and purposeful. By seizing on my interest in the native flora and fauna, she made it relevant. The real beauty of the entire experience was that she did it intuitively, without any formal education or "interpretive" experience.

Imagine what you can do if you go into an interpretive opportunity with training!

—L.B.

mating rituals of prairie chickens, dance can be a hands-on (or feet-on) way to bring your message alive. Many cultures have used interpretive dances to tell the stories of their homelands, lifestyles, or ancestry. The deer dance performed by the Ballet Folklorico de México is a compelling and powerful expression of a hunting culture that simply cannot be communicated with the same intensity in a slide show or discussion format. Its haunting music and visual poetry can change forever the way one views deer hunting and those who must do it to survive. The message is clear and unforgettable, delivered without a single word spoken.

Experiment with performance skills to find something that fits your personal style. Many interpreters find the use of puppets or costumed characters allows them to say and do things that would otherwise be difficult to demonstrate. Becoming a "living tree" that walks and talks may help audiences connect with the concept of photosynthesis far better than viewing a chart on the effects of sunlight on plants. Simple hand puppets allow skunks, frogs, or even cardboard boxes to tell their own stories and can help people see previously unloved species in a new light. Learning about snakes from an overstuffed snake puppet might be just what someone with a fear of snakes needs before mustering the courage to view or touch the real thing.

Slide and Multimedia Programs

Slide programs are one of the standards in the interpreter's tool kit. But like everything else, there's an appropriate way and an inappropriate way to use them. Inappropriate would be the cruise director who says as you board, "We have a program tonight you won't want to miss. I'll be showing all 240 of my slides from my last trip to Jamaica. It'll take about two hours, but most of them are really great pictures!" Even if you're interested in Jamaica, it's doubtful you'll leave that program with anything other than a roaring headache. More appropriate would be the guide who welcomes you to their program, then uses thirty to eighty excellent slides to illustrate a half-hour thematic presentation.

With modern technology, the slide projector with its carousel of slides might be going the way of the dinosaur, yet many interpreters still use them. If you're not yet using a computerized version of a slide program like Microsoft PowerPoint™, you should take time to become familiar with the slide projector before your program debuts. Most projectors have the cord attached and coiled inside a compartment. Once you get it plugged in, check to make sure the light bulb is working. Keep a spare light bulb on hand at all times and know how to change it before it becomes necessary. Your audience doesn't want to learn this skill if you're having to fumble through it during one of your presentations. Clean the lens and practice focusing. If you have a remote cable (or an electronic cableless remote) that allows you to change slides from a distance, use it. Make sure any connections are tight and that the remote is functioning prior to the program. Set up well in advance of your program, before audience members arrive and run through the entire carousel to ensure that all your slides are in order and facing the correct direction. Slides go in the carousel upside down and backwards, so it's easy to make mistakes. And although such mistakes are sometimes entertaining, they detract from the professionalism of your program and are easily avoided with a little forethought.

If you have access to a computer projection system and slide program software, follow the instructions for setting up and displaying your slides. Again, remember to set up ahead of time and run through the entire program to catch any glitches. With either setup, be prepared for the inevitable equipment failure. Your program should be able to stand alone, without the images, if necessary. In spite of all your preparations, anything that plugs into an outlet is subject to mechanical failure, and it seems be a law of nature that it will happen at the most inconvenient time possible. Whichever system you use, here are a few tips that might make your program a little more enjoyable for the audience.

Use only the best images in your slides. If you have to apologize for a slide's quality or explain what the photo is because it isn't clear enough, don't use it. Check the Internet or computer clip-art catalogs for professional-quality images. Make sure the images make sense for your presentation. Don't use a sunset picture of cacti just because it's beautiful if your presentation is about rain forests. Be aware of copyright issues. Some resources on the Internet are free for you to use. Others require paying the photographer or artist for the use. Don't assume that no

Left: Wallace Keck of Arkansas State Parks guides visitors into the forests and fields to learn about the importance and uses of native wildflowers. Photo courtesy of Arkansas State Parks. Right: Interpreters at Walt Disney World's Animal Kingdom bring animals like this corn snake up close where children and adults can learn about them in the safety and comfort of a controlled situation. Photo by Tim Merriman. Far right: A National Park Service interpreter at Cape Cod National Seashore makes the story of cranberry farming more tangible by demonstrating the tools of the trade while dressed in typical attire of the period. Photo by Tim Merriman.

one in your audience will know the difference. Someone may know the photograph or the artwork and want an explanation. It's better to get permission to use illustrations or find ones that are available at no charge.

When you set up your program, insert a black or blank slide at the beginning and end. This allows you to have the slide projector running and ready to go during your introduction, but without a blinding white screen facing your audience. It's especially important to end with a black slide rather than a white screen so that the audience's pupils aren't suddenly forced to constrict after becoming accustomed to the previous, darker slides. Similarly, if you want to put "divider" slides in the body of your program, use blank or dark title slides rather than leaving a blank space in the carousel.

Avoid looking at the screen during your presentation. You should already know what's up there, so talk to your audience, not the slide. It's all right to sneak a peek at each slide as it comes up on the screen, just to provide yourself a mental cue or assure yourself that the slide is displayed properly, but then refocus immediately on your audience. Aside from being more polite, it helps the audience hear you better if your voice is directed at them instead of being absorbed by the screen.

Avoid describing the slide ("This is a deer"). Your audience can see what's on the screen. And the reality is that the slide is a picture of a deer, not the deer itself. If you think it's boring to go on a guided walk and have the guide point out every plant and tell you its name, just wait until you go through that process with slides. It's an annoying habit that every interpreter falls into unless he or she is vigilant, so make a practice of avoiding the words *This is a...* and you should be just fine. Unless there's a specific reason to point to something on the slide, use your words to direct attention to the image rather than walking to the screen and touching it. Again, it's a matter of directing your attention and your voice to the audience as opposed to the screen.

When deciding how many slides to use, figure one slide for about every eight seconds. Actual on-screen time should depend on the content of the slide and the point you're making, but generally slides should be on no fewer than six seconds or more than ten. In a typical twenty-minute presentation, you might use three to five minutes for your introductory statements, then show twenty to forty slides for about five to ten minutes during the body of the program, then move on to your conclusion and question period for the remaining five to ten minutes. During your introductory and concluding statements, be sure the light level in the room is high enough to allow the audience to see you. Ideally you should be illuminated during the entire presentation, but make sure that the light level allows the slides to be seen clearly or there's not much point in having them.

One of the simplest ways to develop a slide program is to create storyboard cards. These simple three-inch-by-five-inch index cards can help you plan and practice your presentation, but don't use them during the show. For each slide you want to use, create a card that has the words or thought that will accompany that slide. You might even want to do a quick stick-figure sketch of the slide in the corner of the card. Lay out the cards on a table and rearrange as needed to help you develop your theme and communicate your subthemes. Once you have them in the right order, it's easy to create transition statements that take you from one image or thought to the next. Number the cards, and then load your carousel (or your PowerPoint™ presentation) correspondingly, and you're all set. Use the cards to practice your presentation, even when it's not convenient to have your slides in front of you. Then leave the cards behind when it's time to do the program. If you must use notes, make them small and inconspicuous, and use as few as you possibly can.

Multimedia presentations can be interesting if done well. Done badly, they make the audience very aware of the technology and the theme gets lost.

Presentations with PowerPoint™ can have some added elements of interest if you are a budding "techie" and willing to learn the more advanced techniques. These computer-based presentations can include video clips, music, and quotes. It takes practice to make the program work well, but it can be saved easily and used again later or adapted to a new situation.

Digital cameras offer another interesting opportunity. You can take photos of your group while hiking or touring and incorporate them into a PowerPoint™ presentation later that evening. People enjoy this "instant celebrity" feeling, and it personalizes a medium that might otherwise seem cold. A digital camera also allows quick and easy photographs or maps or artifacts too fragile to be handled.

You can also purchase a slide adapter for some of the new digital cameras that makes it easy to digitize photos from slides you have. Most photos project best at 150-dots-per-inch resolution. Photo-editing programs allow you to prepare the photos at the desired resolution and even improve the lighting or contrast of the image for a particular use. This is a considerable advantage over slides, which cannot easily be improved.

Running through the show before guests arrive not only tests the equipment and lighting situation, it preloads the images in the volatile memory of the computer and makes them project more quickly when you go back through the show with your audience. High-tech shows are not for everyone, but exciting opportunities exist for those who truly enjoy learning the nuances of these new technologies.

Demonstrations

Incorporating a demonstration into your program can be an effective way of making a point and provides an opportunity for audience interaction. For example, instead of simply telling your audience how to put on a personal flotation device, you can demonstrate it by having an audience member try one on. Adjust the fit, and then have another audience member test the device. If you plan to use a demonstration, make sure it's appropriate to your theme and the overall content of your presentation. Avoid demonstrations that add nothing but a bit of flash to the program. Demonstrating a magic trick may be fun and entertaining, but if it doesn't relate to the purpose of the program, it doesn't belong.

Demonstrations generally work best if the group is relatively small—between ten and twenty people—or when the group is seated in a setting where everyone has a good view. Use large objects to ensure that all audience members can see what you're demonstrating. If your demonstration involves something smaller than a tennis ball, pass it around the group so that everyone has a good look at the object and a chance to ask questions.

Invite the audience to become part of the demonstration whenever possible, but be sure their safety is considered (don't, for example, ask a novice diver to demonstrate the use of breathing apparatus underwater). Test all the parts involved in your demonstration prior to the presentation to make sure they work and that you know how to use them. Be prepared for the audience member who tries but can't repeat the demonstration. Make sure each person enjoys the failed effort just as much as if he or she had performed brilliantly.

If you plan to use live animals as a part of your program, consider leaving them hidden while you deliver your introduction and perhaps even some of the body of the program. Once an animal takes the stage, you run the risk of the audience diverting all their attention to the creature, especially if it's cute, large, noisy, or compelling to look at in any other way. If simply watching the animal is the aim of your program, then you will have succeeded, but if you're trying to get across important concepts and want the animal to reinforce those concepts, you will do well to bring the beast out after your point has had the chance to be heard.

Be aware that some animals may be somewhat scary for people, even if the majority of the audience thinks otherwise. Respect the fears of your individual audience members, and never force someone to touch or handle an animal or make fun of them for being afraid. If you're able to change someone's fearful attitude during the course of your program, give yourself a gold star, but understand that many people have deep-seated concerns that you cannot overcome in the space of a half-hour presentation.

Whenever you handle live animals in an audience situation, pay special attention to safety issues, both for the animal and the audience.

Activities

Demonstrations generally show how something works and may involve just one or two audience members. Activities, on the other hand, usually involve multiple members of the audience, are generally more gamelike, and help people understand concepts. Activities embedded in your program can appeal to all age groups but, if they are poorly planned, they can simply disrupt the flow of your program rather than helping you make your point.

Before incorporating an activity into your program, test it with colleagues or family members before trying it with an audience. Activities might include scavenger hunts, childhood games modified to illustrate a concept (for example, a game of tag adapted to show how bats hunt moths by echolocation), or simple crafts. Seek out a variety of sources of appropriate activities to increase your bag of tricks. Books like Joseph Cornell's *Sharing Nature with Children* (1998. Nevada City, CA: Dawn Publishing) are an excellent resource. Also check web sites of related organizations, visit your library for activity ideas, or adapt scout or school activities to illustrate your theme. Outline activities on note cards or a computer database and keep a file handy so you can look them up later. Use a keyword to code the activities so that it will be easy to find activities related to your program's theme.

If the activity doesn't support or illustrate your theme, don't use it. There's little point in developing an activity for the sake of being active. Even if you're using the activity as a transition or time killer for a group of squirming eight-year-olds, it's advisable to adapt the activity to reflect your theme. Take every chance you can to reinforce your message.

Gather all supplies needed to conduct the activity well before the presentation. Plan for extras in case your audience is larger than anticipated. Try to use supplies that are expendable so that breakage won't be an issue. If your supplies reflect the theme, so much the better. If, for example, you're doing a program about recycling, use only recyclable supplies or be prepared to explain that your supplies are a negative example.

Give clear instructions to audience members. Practicing the activity before your presentation with colleagues or family who have never done it will be a good test for your instructions. Be prepared to help those who don't understand your instructions or who are unable to participate fully due to a disability, but don't ignore the rest of your audience. It helps to have a backup activity that can quickly replace your planned activity if one or more audience members is clearly unable to participate.

Guided Tours

Sometimes it's appropriate to take your program from place to place, such as in a historic house tour or along a nature trail. Guided tours can also be done from horseback, in canoes or kayaks, or in buses, vans, trains, trams, or other modes of transportation. Many of these types of tours have traditionally been considered recreational, but there's no reason that a recreation excursion can't also be an interpretive opportunity. So no matter how your tour moves from location to location, a few tips can help you keep your group together and focused on your interpretive message.

Start on time and return to the starting point when promised. If you find you are running more than twenty to thirty minutes late at any point, offer some means of allowing audience members to contact those who might be waiting on them. You are the leader of the group, and they depend on you to get them from start to end safely.

Establish a "staging area" where people can gather prior to the tour. This is your chance to meet the group and establish rapport before beginning your presentation. Your presence will indicate the location of the staging area, so be sure to arrive at least ten to fifteen minutes prior to your scheduled program.

Even if you've met everyone informally while the group was forming prior to the tour, take the time to greet them as a group and structure the experience. If you will be mounting horses or getting into canoes or kayaks, deliver your introductory statements, including safety messages, before the audience members get onto or into their individual conveyances.

If you have people who may not be physically up to the challenge of your tour, try to take them aside before you start and explain the physical demands of the tour. Make them feel welcome, but help them make the right choice for their comfort. For example, if you're taking a group on a two-mile hike in rough terrain, check out their shoes discreetly while the group gathers. If you notice someone in high-heeled sandals, suggest quietly that they may be more comfortable if they stay behind. Some guide companies suggest pretesting your audience for physically challenging tours. If you're offering tours delivered in kayaks or on horseback, you may need to assess the individual's ability to participate before you head down the river or trail. Try to do so in a way that is sensitive to the individual's needs, but be firm so that you don't put yourself or other visitors at risk during the tour.

After your introductory statements (usually delivered at the staging area), move out briskly for the first stop, then set a moderate pace to the remaining stops. Stay ahead of your group between stops. You are their leader, and it's up to you to signal when to stop. Otherwise you may find that you are having to call the group back when you stop. Check to make sure that your group is comfortable with the pace that you set. If you have laggards, adjust your pace accordingly. If you have a very large group or are leading a high-risk group (horseback riders or kayakers), it's a good idea to have a second guide along to bring up the rear and ensure that no one gets lost along the way.

If possible, make your first stop within sight of your starting point so that latecomers can join you. Be prepared to welcome others who might want to join your group along the way. If there's a reason for them not to join your tour (perhaps they haven't paid, your group is already too large, or you're leading a special tour), be prepared to suggest politely but firmly that they need to move along or return to the ticket booth or whatever other response is most appropriate.

When you stop, make sure the entire group has gathered at the stop and everyone is focused on you before you begin speaking. This may mean that you need to wait several seconds before conversations between audience members die down, but usually, if you just wait quietly, attention will return to you fairly quickly. When you begin speaking, use a conversational tone of voice, but be sure that you are speaking loudly enough to be heard by every member of the group.

If an audience member makes a comment or asks a question, repeat the question or comment before answering so that everyone can hear what was asked. Alternatively, you can rephrase the question in your response. For example, if someone asks how often pelicans feed, you can either repeat the question and then answer it, or you can say something such as, "Pelicans feed all day long."

Think about what you can say at the end of a stop as a transition to the next stop. You may want to use mystery as a way to engage the guest in thinking about what lies ahead down the trail or around the bend on the lake's shore. You might say, "We had an interesting glimpse of where Native Americans lived under this shelter bluff. But they must have needed a water supply. Help me watch for places where they might have found a ready source of clean water." Then when you approach the spring along the bluff, you will have guests who are already thinking about its purpose. Your first sentence can tie into the transition sentence from the previous stop. "You've probably guessed that this spring was their water supply, but what could they have used to transport the water?" Your stimulating question following the transition statement will engage them quickly in studying surroundings for potential water containers.

As you explore on your tour, take advantage of "teachable moments" when something out of the ordinary occurs, even if it doesn't relate to your theme. If it doesn't relate to your theme, you don't need to dwell on the event, but you should not ignore a bald eagle stealing a fish from an osprey within two hundred feet of the group, even if the original program had more to do with plants. It's fine to take a quick poll of your group and see if they mind stopping to view a spectacular event, even if it means throwing the tour off schedule temporarily. Most will welcome the chance to see a right whale feeding or bull elk locking antlers by the side of the road. These unforgettable opportunities are what define peak experiences for audience members, and it's likely the glacier will still be there if you arrive fifteen minutes later. On the other hand, use your best judgment to avoid creating schedule problems that might seriously affect your audience members. Missed flights or hotel reservations might not be appreciated, even if the trade-off is a once-in-a-lifetime viewing opportunity.

When you come to the end of your tour, have a definite dismissal point. This is the place where you'll deliver your concluding statements. It's a great time to restate the theme, the main message for your tour. Be friendly as you end the program, but make it clear the show is over. Thank everyone for attending, and offer to stay for ten to fifteen minutes to answer additional questions. Invite the audience to join you again sometime and to tell their friends about your program. This is your last and best chance to make a good impression and to leave them smiling.

Recommended Reading

Lewis, William J. 1980. *Interpreting for Park Visitors*. Fort Washington, PA: Eastern National.

Writing a Program Outline

The previous chapters detailed the elements that help to make an interpretive presentation successful. Now it's time to put it all together into an outline that will act as the road map for your program. Use the outline to organize your thinking and to practice your presentation. If you feel you must keep notes with you during your program, condense the outline to a few key words that will jog your memory with just a glance. The following items should be included in your outline.

Goal

In Chapter 4, you learned that the programs you do should support the goals of your organization. Start your program outline by defining which goal or goals your program will address.

Objectives

Now get a little more specific. Include at least one measurable objective in the outline. What will the audience do differently after participating in your program? What will they learn, and how will you be able to know if they learned it? Writing the objective(s) helps you articulate a cause-effect relationship. If you are successful in delivering the message, or theme, the described action will be the result. You may have more than one objective for a presentation, but try to limit yourself to two objectives or you may be expecting too much from your audience.

Theme

State your theme in a single sentence that says specifically what you want your audience to understand. You may be able to use the key words in your theme to come up with an attention-getting title that will

Above: An umbrella used by this guide at Qinxi Gardens in Chengdu, Sichuan, China, is a better choice for shade on a sunny day than sunglasses because it allows her to make eye contact with her audience. Photo by Tim Merriman. Left: This Walt Disney World interpreter has chosen a very approachable setting to interpret tarantulas. The larger-than-scale model allows him to point out traits of the spider more easily than with the living animal in the box. The portable microphone allows him to use his hands for the demonstration and still project his voice to audiences that can grow to forty or more people. Photo by Tim Merriman.

draw people to your program. See Chapter 4 if you need to review the components of a theme.

Introduction

In Chapter 5, you learned the value of a good introduction. The introduction will offer the first opportunity for you to tell the audience your theme. You may want to write out a couple of introductory sentences on your presentation outline to help you organize your thoughts. You won't be using your outline during your presentation, but if you take the time to write out your introductory statements, they will be easier to remember at show time.

Body

The body of the talk contains the three to five subthemes, or message elements, you developed in preparation for your presentation. Listing those subthemes on your outline will remind you of the points you want to make. For each subtheme, list any supporting activities you want to use. If you're going to use your outline

National Park Service interpreters at Dinosaur National Monument interpret the past in the relative comfort of a visitor center built over this important paleontological site. Photo by Tim Merriman.

during your presentation, underline the activities to serve as a quick reminder.

Conclusion

The outline should contain your closing restatement of the theme. This is your last chance to make your point. State it on the outline exactly as you hope to deliver it and practice it often. You may want to deliver the theme in slightly different words than you did in the introduction for greater impact. Sometimes a quote that expresses the theme is a powerful and memorable way to restate it in the conclusion.

Materials or Other Resources Needed

The outline should also have a key list of other materials or resources you will use in the presentation. If a field guide and binoculars are essential, you want them on the outline as a reminder. If you have an extensive list of props or supplies, package them in a kit and just remind yourself in the outline to bring "the kit." You don't want to be assembling complex program supplies just a few minutes before going to speak. Have that done well in advance, and just use the outline to remind you what must go with you.

It's always a good idea to have a Plan B as an alternative if something unpredictable occurs. Make a note of your Plan B in case weather, mechanical failures, or other unforeseen disasters interrupt your Plan A.

Setting the Stage

You've got it all down on paper. You've thought through your presentation and now it's show time. Sound scary? If you're like most interpreters, you might have to talk yourself into getting in front of the group, but once you're there and launched into your program, you'll be just fine. To help make things a little easier, try to create the optimum setting for your presentation, so you and your audience will feel more comfortable.

Remember Maslow's Hierarchy (see Chapter 3)? Check your program setting to see if it will meet the basic physiological needs of you and your audience. Is the temperature comfortable? If not, are there ways to make it more comfortable? If you're indoors, the thermostat should provide relief. If you're outdoors, look for shady spots to deliver your messages if it's hot or places out of the wind if it's cold. Although your own comfort is important, the comfort of your audience is more important. Be aware of your positioning, especially on sunny outdoor hikes. Keep your audience facing away from the sun, so they can direct their attention to you instead of to keeping the glare out of their eyes.

For short presentations of an hour or two, you probably don't need to worry about providing food and drink, but refreshments always make guests feel more comfortable and cared for. If going on longer outings or daylong tours or programs, plan ahead for how your visitors will find refreshment. Check out the shortest route to the nearest restroom facility so you can advise your visitors of its location.

Find the best location from which you can address the audience. Standing behind a podium in an auditorium may work for a classroom lecture, but most interpretive audiences will feel more comfortable with an informal approach. Set up your visual aids and make sure they can be seen clearly from every audience angle. If your group is large, be sure to position yourself so that everyone can see you. If you're on a trail, stepping up onto a rock or other elevated ground might raise you just enough so the people in the back of the group can hear you easily. Check with the audience periodically, either verbally or visually, to make sure that everyone can see and hear you. Take the time to scope out the best locations in your presentation room or along the trail before your group arrives, and your audience will thank you for it.

Helpful Hints
Overcoming Fear

Fear can be a good thing. It can motivate people to accomplish extraordinary feats they would otherwise be incapable of achieving. Fear stimulates your adrenal glands, speeds up your heart rate, and gives you an edge. But there's a point at which the positive aspects of fear begin to backslide behind an avalanche of negative emotion. The key to overcoming fear is to learn to recognize and walk that fine line between energizing anxiety and outright terror. Then you begin to use your fear instead of letting it use you.

Remember that your audience is made up of people just like you. They laugh and cry and act silly sometimes. They have families and pets and hobbies and problems. We're really not very different after all, when it comes right down to it. Interpretive audiences are looking for a good time, and while they may consider you an authority on your subject matter, they also view you as a person. They want you to relax and have a good time right along with them. They want you to succeed. So if you get so nervous or tongue-tied that your audience is aware of it, making a joke of it will usually put them and you at ease and your program back on track.

Know your material. Most of the fear we experience in speaking before a group is caused by that sneaking suspicion that we don't really know as much as we think we do. We're afraid that someone will expose our ignorance or that we'll forget everything we ever knew as soon as we get past our name. The reality is that no interpreter can ever know all there is to know about a given subject. You shouldn't even pretend that you do. Ideally you know enough to be comfortable in your presentation and enough to recognize what you don't know. If new at a job, Bill Lewis, author of *Interpreting for Park Visitors,* recommends that you get well acquainted with the organization's general brochure for the public. It usually contains 90 percent of the essential information about interpreting the area.

If someone asks for more detail than you have on hand, simply admit that you're not sure and direct them to another source of information. Sometimes someone in the audience will offer up the information. Avoid the impulse to ignore or correct them for stepping on your lines. Instead, embrace the information they have to offer and help put it into perspective for your audience.

Practice your presentation. Run through your program from start to finish several times to increase your comfort level. Take it for a test ride in front of your colleagues or family to see if it all makes sense. Tweak it till it feels right, but avoid memorizing a script. Scripted speeches sound stilted and get stale quickly. Worse, if you forget the script, you're likely to get flustered and confused. If you lose your place, you lose your audience as well. A better approach is to practice the order of your key points but leave the exact wording to unfold in spontaneous reaction to the audience's interest. If certain phrases seem to elicit a desired reaction, try to remember them for the next time, but don't worry over getting every word exactly the same in every presentation, or your audience will be as bored as you are boring.

Get wrapped up in your passion for the subject matter. Once you begin to speak from the heart and see that your audience is engaged in the presentation, your fear will simply disappear. In fact, you may find that you just want to take the audience on home with you because you've become so close through sharing your love of the topic.

Nonverbal Communication

In *Hamlet,* William Shakespeare says that "one may smile, and smile, and be a villain." It's true that you can sometimes paint on a smile, regardless of what's in your heart, but your overall body language often conveys a message completely different from what you thought you said with words. Nonverbal communication is a critical part of your interpretive presentation. With your posture, your attitude, and facial expressions, you either welcome people or let them know you're too busy for them.

Remember the last time you were at a department store? You had a question about a potential purchase, but the sales clerk was on the phone with her boyfriend and clearly not interested in helping you until she'd attended to her own needs. She even turned her back slightly, refused to look you in the eye, and kept her voice low so you would know you were intruding on her personal conversation. Her body language spoke volumes, and she never had to say a word to you. In fact, you couldn't have gotten her to say a word to you. So you gave up in frustration and left the store without making the purchase.

When you slouch or sigh, fold your arms or roll your eyes, you give out signals to your audience. They've come to buy into your interpretive message, and you've just told them you're not interested in helping them find what they need. If you show up in a soiled uniform or tattered field clothes, you've let them know you don't respect them enough to keep yourself neat and clean. Remember that you represent an agency or a company that wants repeat business. How often do you think you'd go back to the same store if the sales clerk continued to ignore you or frightened you with her unfriendly behavior or hostile appearance?

Stand in front of a mirror or videotape yourself as you run through your program. Check your posture and your facial expressions to ensure that they welcome people and invite participation. Give yourself points if you smile frequently and make eye contact. Look at what you do with your hands and feet. Avoid scratching yourself, rocking back and forth, or pacing like a tiger in the zoo. These body movements are distracting and don't add to the program. Practice standing naturally and using your body as a natural extension of your voice. When you have a strong point to make, open your arms wide. If you're whispering for emphasis, keep your hands closer in to your body. Just act naturally, and your body will automatically help you make your point without seeming contrived

Keep your hair out of your face. It doesn't need to be pulled back severely, but if your hair tends to fall in your eyes, it will mask your expression and make it difficult to establish or maintain eye contact. If you have shoulder-length hair or longer, you might want to consider pulling it back into a ponytail, especially if you're going to be outside on windy days. Nothing's worse than trying to speak through a mouthful of hair, unless it's trying to listen to someone trying to speak through a mouthful of hair.

Avoid wearing excessive amounts of jewelry. Simple rings, earrings, and necklaces might be fine if they don't violate your organization's dress code, but elaborate jewelry and multiple bangle bracelets, dangling earrings, and unusual body piercings are distracting and may even be dangerous if you suddenly find yourself in a rescue situation. Save these items for after-hours wear. Some organizations tell guides that they will not be allowed on the floor with guests if they are dressed to be more appealing than the exhibits and the site. Interpreters are often asked to wear uniforms or not wear the extras so that guests understand that you are there to help them enjoy the resource. You are not there to be the attraction.

If you wear sunglasses on sunny days, take them off when speaking. Making eye contact is important, and sunglasses remove your ability to express yourself in very important ways. It is often said that you never get a second chance to make a first impression. Be aware that your appearance, body language, attitude, and voice project messages as well or better than the spoken word. It is also said that 10 percent of communication is what you say and 90 percent is how you say it. As professionals, you want to be effective communicators on all levels and in every way.

Voice Modulation

You can't all be James Earl Jones with a mellifluous baritone sought after for feature film voice-overs, but you can work with what you have to develop a pleasant and expressive speaking voice. What you're after is variety in pitch, tone, volume, and speed. Variety breathes life into a presentation and holds the interest of the audience. Listen to a monotone or someone whose voice never changes from an annoying pattern, like always lilting up at the end of a sentence so that each statement becomes a question. In either case, you're looking for the nearest exit within sixty seconds. If you can't find one, it's like being in a closed room with someone dragging their fingernails across a blackboard. Repeatedly.

A videotape or audiotape of your presentation is one of the easiest ways to tell if your voice is varied enough to hold audience interest. If not, look for places where speeding up, slowing down, getting louder, or even whispering might create appropriate emphasis and help you make your point.

If you have a pronounced accent, try to soften it but not eliminate it. An accent is part of what makes you a unique individual. However, some accents are difficult to listen to or understand. Regionalisms (Texans are always "fixin' to" do something) can add local color to your presentation, but make sure you're not using regional vocabulary that your audience may not understand unless you take the time to explain the unfamiliar words.

Practice enunciating difficult and commonly mispronounced words. No one expects your diction to be perfect, but if you frequently mispronounce words, you will lose credibility with your audience. If someone takes the time to correct your pronunciation after your presentation, thank him or her. Chances are good he or she is absolutely right, and you would do well to take the correction in a spirit of self-improvement rather than taking offense.

Registers of Voice

Can you recall times when you have spoken politely to someone on the phone, and then covered the mouthpiece so you could yell the message to a friend in a very familiar tone? Or you read a story to a child, and soon you were portraying the bear in the story with your own gruff voice as the bear speaks? We all do this routinely. We have a phone voice, an informal tone for family members, a more formal one for our supervisor or a professor, and we switch from one to the other from sentence to sentence.

These registers of voice are useful tools in programs when you deliver quotes, tell stories, or read from a well-written book. With some practice it is easy to develop a different voice or register for a character in the story. You can sound more masculine or feminine, younger or older, and have a regional accent as a character. Using varied registers adds interest for your audience. Don't be afraid to experiment with it when appropriate.

Whispering is used by many storytellers to emphasize important passages. Children and adults will lean forward and listen more carefully to hear what you say.

Reading aloud to your children, friends, or family members from storybooks or fairy tales is a great way to practice. Allow yourself to become each different character with voice and expressions. Then when the opportunity arises to tell a story in a program, use vocal registers to bring it all alive for your audience. Like kids listening to their favorite bedtime story, your audience will be enthralled.

Using Humor or Anecdotes

Humor is part of the human condition, which might lead you to think that it's always appropriate to be funny. Unfortunately, what's humorous to one person might not be so clever to someone else. In fact, some people might be offended by a specific joke or a joking manner. For some, a jokester is someone who lacks respect for the audience. Using humor in a personal presentation can be a bit tricky, to find a balance between universal humor and personal affront. If you aren't blessed with a naturally overdeveloped sense of humor, you would do well simply to play things straight instead of trying to spice up your program with forced jokes.

In any case, avoid jokes that poke fun of individuals or groups of people, even if you personally find the jokes enjoyable. Similarly, avoid humorous comments about religion or politics. Instead, look for the irony of a situation or put a new twist on looking at things. Remember, you're there to convey a message, not to get laughs. If the laughter comes spontaneously, that's a bonus.

Using foreign accents can be effective if you are from the ethnic group being portrayed. However, be aware that it may be offensive to people you are trying to portray when you do it badly or when they perceive you as making fun of their culture. Humor created in this way can backfire and alienate guests.

If you're not comfortable using humor in your programs, think about using personal anecdotes or stories of famous people to illustrate your points. Storytelling is a natural interpretive tool and one which can be used to great effect. Keep the stories short and to the point. Make sure they relate directly to your program's theme and aren't just a time-filler.

Recommended Reading

Knudson, Douglas M., Ted T. Cable, and Larry Beck. 1995. *Interpretation of Cultural and Natural Resources.* Chapter 19. State College, PA: Venture Publishing, Inc.

Lewis, William J. 1991. *Interpreting for Park Visitors.* Chapter 8. Fort Washington, PA: Eastern National.

Personal Contacts

You are working the information desk of a visitor center, roving a nature trail, standing in the new exhibit at a museum, or hanging out on the deck of a cruise boat. All of these circumstances are wonderful informal interpretation opportunities. People talk to you casually and ask questions. In many ways, this interaction is the most powerful chance for an interpreter to make a real difference with the audience. You are engaged in communication one to one or with just a few people at a time, and your focus can be on their specific questions and interests. You no longer have a generalized audience, requiring the more general approaches we've discussed for organized interpretive programs.

Knowledge of your audience is important in every interpretive setting. In the informal setting, you can ask questions that help you understand the needs of the people. A few important questions at the start might be: How much time do you have? Have you been here before? Are you new to bird watching, whale watching, wildflower walks? Was there something specific you wanted to see or do while here? Would you like some suggestions of other things to do?

When you have enough knowledge of their interests, time limits, and concerns, you can shape what you do and say to meet their needs and expectations. First and foremost is to respect their priorities. If they stopped at your desk to ask a quick question, answer the question and allow them to leave. You can always answer a purely informational question with, "And please stop back later if you want to learn more about the park or some programs we offer this weekend." That response takes only a few seconds. There's no need to inflict interpretation on someone who clearly isn't interested at the time.

Sometimes you can answer their simple question

about the location of restrooms or availability of a map and find out their other needs. You might ask, "Do you need any help finding our trails or other things to do while you're here?" Often a guest will ask you a question just to open a dialogue. They may have many questions but are unsure whether it's appropriate to take your time in asking them. Your assurance that you are there to assist them brings on the conversation. It can all start with a quick question about facilities and end up with the guest returning for a program, looking at an exhibit with great interest, or acquiring a brochure or book that will enhance their experiences.

The goal with any informal exchange is to create an interpretive opportunity for the guest that might not happen otherwise. As the interpreter, you are continually in this situation at most jobs. You can try different strategies for engaging guests in trying something new to see what works. It is always exciting when you are able to show them something unique that the guests would have missed without your assistance.

Disengagement

Disengaging from guests during informal interpretive situations is an art of its own. If you are roving on a trail or in a museum, or standing on the deck of a cruise boat, your job may be to be available to all guests, so it's critical that you don't become the private tour guide of one person or couple while neglecting others. Occasionally a guest will simply dominate your time and make it challenging to pull away without being rude. It is always reasonable to say, "Please excuse me while I check on other guests. I'll be back if time permits. Let me know if you have other questions later." You need to keep moving if your proximity to the domineering guest makes it unlikely that others will approach you.

Interpretive Log Book

The *Interpretive Log Book,* developed by the National Park Service in Module 102 of its Interpretive Development Program curriculum, is one way to evaluate informal interpretation and coach guides and interpreters. It is available on the Internet at www.nps.gov/idp/interp/102/index.htm. You can use it to evaluate your personal skills with informal interpretation. The questions provide a way of thinking back through circumstances where you might have led someone to an interpretive opportunity when they asked a simple question of you. If you supervise other guides or interpreters, it can also be used as a coaching tool. You can ask workers to fill it out for three or four typical encounters and then discuss what's been written.

Use the log book concept to evaluate a variety of exchanges with guests. Filling out five to eight logs will provide a range of experiences from brief encounters to more complex ones, perhaps even revealing circumstances when the guest did not seem happy with the result or an opportunity was missed. Just filling out the form helps you self-evaluate the way you're handling your visitors. Getting another person's perspective, such as a trainer or supervisor, adds another layer of value.

We recommend you use the following points to create a form on which you

Contact areas, like this one at Walt Disney World's Animal Kingdom, create a unique opportunity for guests to get acquainted with animals in a friendly, informal situation. Photo by Tim Merriman.

Seizing the Moment

When I was a state park interpreter in Illinois in the 1970s, my favorite vacation was a trip to Florida and the Everglades. We would watch birds and hike in the daytime and road run at night to look for herps (snakes, lizards, turtles, salamanders, and frogs). The roads through wetlands in Florida were famous for the herpetofauna found there. One day we stopped at Corkscrew Swamp Sanctuary, a facility of the National Audubon Society. Their boardwalk trails through the cypress-tupelo swamps were wonderful. They give quiet access to remote locations, usually only reached by wading or in a boat.

At a rest area along the trail, I walked toward an elderly gentleman, seemingly resting. When he saw me, he smiled and pointed off to his left. I looked where he pointed, and a handsome barred owl stared back from only six feet off the trail, roosting on a low limb. I had a telephoto lens and took many photos up close of the engaging bird. The old gentleman told me many interesting things about barred owls, and I was impressed with his knowledge and willingness to share what he knew.

After the hike, I returned to the visitor center and asked who the old gent was. They said, "Alexander Sprunt, Jr.," one of their volunteers. I had just read Mr. Sprunt's book, *Birds of Prey,* and was excited to know I had met him. I went back onto the trail, found Mr. Sprunt, and thanked him for his book and the wonderful story in it about "mouse reproduction" and the importance of predators. I still tell the mouse story thirty years later. Mr. Sprunt's ability to create an interpretive opportunity by showing me an owl I would have missed was another lesson. He knew how to let the animal be the catalyst, but he was still available with smiles and stories to be the guide and interpreter.

—*T.M.*

can record each encounter. You may respond using either full paragraphs or short answers. Be sure to address all applicable topics. You may use either a narrative format or a short-answer format for your logs.

Describe the audience interaction in your own words, making sure to include all applicable points. Simply type or write answers to these questions for each guest encounter in an informal setting:

- Location—where did the guest exchange take place?
- Audience—how would you describe the guest (age, gender, interests)?
- How was the episode initiated?
- Time constraints—how long did the interaction last?
- Special circumstances—were guests ill, angry, etc.?
- What was your perception of the guest's needs?
- How did you determine these needs?
- What response options were available?
- Which option did you select and why?
- What sources supported the chosen option (policies, regulations, research material)?
- How did the visitor respond?
- What follow-up questions did you ask, and why?
- How did your responses enhance the audience's experience?
- How did this progression move the audience closer to an interpretive opportunity?

Using a Log Book for NAI Certification

NAI's Certified Heritage Interpreter (CHI) category requires that you submit two evidences of performance in addition to a video of a presentation. For those working in the cruise or tour industry, this can be difficult if you do not often have the opportunity to develop nonpersonal interpretive media. NAI allows you to use a collection of eight interpretive logs as a submission in lieu of one of the two required evidences of performance. You still have to come up with one nonpersonal evidence (exhibit design, interpretive signs, brochure) to submit, but the log book of eight encounters may be submitted in the CHI process.

If you do plan to use an interpretive log book in this way, keep in mind:

- Choose eight that show a variety of kinds of guest contacts.
- Don't be afraid to include one or two that don't seem "successful."
- Be sure to document what the guest says in response to your efforts.
- Fill out the form soon after the communication with a guest takes place.

Some Approaches Are Better Than Others

The Mormon Church owns and operates a very interesting interpretive site that tells the story of their brief and tragic stay in Illinois. They have restored the historic town of Nauvoo on the Mississippi River, and they operate a very nice visitor center on the property. In the mid-1970s I visited there and had a memorable experience with their interpretive programs. It was the best I had seen and very nearly the worst. In the restored historic village, retired Mormon elders work as volunteer interpreters. We stopped at the print shop and met a charming elderly couple who had worked their entire lives as printers. Their knowledge of the printing process, passion for the work, and love for their church made it a very pleasant experience. It was especially nice that they seemed to respect their secular audience and only relate the theological sides of their messages if requested. They had just the right touch with informally interpreting the village to us.

After a leisurely visit with several Mormon elder couples in different buildings, we took the visitor center tour. The volunteer guiding our group launched into a guided tour that seemed memorized. When I asked a question during the tour, he gave a less than complete answer and then tried to pick up on his talk. After a moment of frustration, he admitted that my question had derailed him. So he started over from the beginning. My fellow tourists glared at me. I had forced them to get a ten-minute repeat of a less than-fascinating presentation on the history of the Mormon Church. And the evangelical message that was not so evident at the village was very evident in this tour. I left with that odd feeling that I wanted to share my good experience at Nauvoo with colleagues but would not encourage anyone to take the visitor center tour. I cannot say that a memorized tour never works, but I cannot think of a circumstance where I have experienced one that seemed personal and valuable. They usually have the appeal of any regurgitated presentation. But I'll never forget Nauvoo and the Mormon story they interpreted so well at the village.

—T.M.

Evaluation Techniques

Next time you attend someone else's interpretive program or tour, take a few minutes to listen to the comments people make to their companions on their way out. You might be surprised that the person who goes up to congratulate the speaker on a job well done is the same person that tells his wife how ridiculous he thought the speaker was, especially when she gave the wrong information to an audience member's question.

If you rely solely on the nice things that people say to your face for your evaluation comments, you will be getting an unrealistic picture of your performance. Few people will take the time to tell you what you've done wrong or make suggestions on how you can improve. They believe you're doing the best you can and so don't want to hurt your feelings if your performance was less than stellar. They may think what you're doing isn't rocket science and it really won't matter if you're not the cream of the crop. But what they may not realize is that if you're doing your job well, it can make a difference in the way people think and feel, and the actions they take. And that may be more important than rocket science.

Establishing a variety of evaluation strategies can provide a more balanced view of your performance. Listen to the nice things that people say to boost your self-confidence, but learn from comments that come in other ways to improve the way you conduct your programs. In a previous chapter, we mentioned videotaping or audiotaping your presentation so you can evaluate your own performance. This approach is a valuable tool, but you might tend to be either overly critical or not critical enough. Have colleagues or family members watch or listen to the tape and share their perspectives, remembering that they might view your performance through their own filters. Your mom's take on things might not be the same as that of your boss, and both of those perspectives will likely be far different than the audience's. On the other hand, your audience is made up of different people with different expectations and levels of tolerance, so getting a variety of perspectives, tempered with your own self-evaluation, can be a powerful tool.

If possible, have someone professionally trained in interpretation tag along on your tour or attend your program. Ask for an objective evaluation of your performance, and then make adjustments as necessary. An observer might be able to point out opportunities for adding more audience interaction or catch technical jargon that the audience may not understand without additional explanation or analogies. It's usually best to have the observer be someone not associated with your site or company. Your co-workers or supervisor may be too close to the subject matter to get a good feel for how the audience interprets your interpretation.

Exit surveys can be done in a number of ways to elicit comments from audience members. You can offer evaluation cards and pencils so audience members can make anonymous comments at the end of the tour. Again, be aware that people are more likely to comment on the positive aspects of your performance, so such comments should be read and appreciated. But the real value will be found in the "areas for improvement."

You can also station someone near the exit with a standard questionnaire. This person will ask departing audience members to answer a few simple questions. While these types of surveys can yield some interesting insights, they can also be difficult to administer. People leaving the program are usually anxious to move on to their next planned event and may not want to take the minute or two to answer questions. And while you're asking one person the questions, several others (perhaps all the others) have already left the area.

If you elect to use either the written comment cards or an interview, keep the options for responses simple, quick, and easy. Exit surveys are not the time for elaborate detail. Think about the information that will be of most value to your situation, and keep the questions to five or fewer.

As a different type of exit survey, you can try indirect observation. Simply have an observer in position to watch and listen to the comments people make as they leave. The results won't be scientifically valid, but they can reveal what people really think in a way that other surveys might not be able to provide. If you try this concept, have someone other than yourself be the observer, if possible. Ask them to jot down some of the comments they hear or behaviors they observe.

Regardless of the type of evaluation strategy you use, keep records of the comments people make and observed behaviors. As you revise and improve your program, track the types of comments you receive and behaviors you observe. No matter how good you get, there will always be some way of reaching someone you haven't tried before. It's virtually impossible to have 100 percent success with every program.

When you began to outline your presentation, you should have developed spe-

A Matter of Perspective

I was asked by the director of a historic house museum to attend one of the house tours anonymously and let him know what I thought of the way his guide staff presented the tour. He told me they had worked hard to develop what he thought was a "pretty good" interpretive program but was anxious to get some professional feedback to see where they could improve. Sadly, my tour experience was not "pretty good." In fact, it had some serious problems, ranging from an abruptly rude response to the first question that was asked at the staging area to a somewhat strange juxtaposition of living-history characters and our perky, polo-shirted guide who made each statement a question by lilting up at the end of the sentence.

It was unquestionably one of the worst historic house tours I've ever attended. The entire audience became more and more uncomfortable as the hour wore on, beginning to roll their eyes and lose interest. Watching their body language and listening to whispered comments, I knew I was not alone in my assessment. And yet, as I was leaving, I heard one of those same audience members say to the guide, "That was the best historic house tour I've ever been on."

I followed that gentleman and his wife on the way to their car. The wife said, "I can't believe you told her that. They were so rude. The whole thing was a waste of time." His response was that he wasn't really referring to the guide or the living-history characters but simply that he felt he'd gotten a long and thorough look at the interior of the mansion instead of the usual cursory glimpse from a hallway. He was interested in artifacts and furnishings, so the guide and the characters became simply something to tolerate. She was more interested in the stories behind the people who lived in the house and she felt shortchanged, as I did.

How could this program have been improved? First, the guide could have used better communication techniques, particularly in the areas of responding to questions and modulating the speaking voice. Second, the living-history characters did little to enhance the experience because they were so out of context with the rest of the tour and didn't give us any different information than Miss Polo Shirt provided. When the group arrived at the door, a costumed butler let us in, indicating that the master and mistress were out, but we could wait in the parlor, where the guide picked us up. I thought I was in for something exciting at this point but rapidly had my hopes dashed. But imagine if the guide had been dressed as a maid who then sneaked us through the house so we could peek while the master and mistress were away. We would have been swept into an adventure that appealed to the universal concept of curiosity. These simple changes could make the difference between a dull, uninspired program full of facts ("This lamp is one hundred years old") and something far more memorable, pleasing the entire audience instead of just the furniture buffs who were able to ignore the interpretive program.

—L.B.

cific, measurable objectives. Now is the time to see if your program has accomplished what it set out to do. Some objectives may be short-term objectives, things you want the audience to understand or do immediately (be able to recite the four uses of a beaver's tail, pick up trash along the beach). This type of objective can be tested during or immediately after the program through questioning or exit surveys.

Other objectives may be more long-term, things you want the audience to do once they leave your program (30 percent return rate, tell a friend, begin recycling efforts at home). Because your audiences scatter to the four winds when you're done with them, it may be difficult to measure your success unless the objectives are written in a way that ensures you can. For instance, if our objective is that 30 percent of your clientele on this tour will return within two years, you can measure that by keeping records of who signs up for the tours and then cross-checking to see if they are repeat customers. Of course, it could take up to two years to see if you've been successful. Whatever evaluative methods you use, remember to keep them measurable. Vague measures of success leave us with false information or no real feedback on how successful our programs are at achieving objectives. When you employ measurable outcomes, and follow up to assess your success, you have an opportunity to improve on ideas that work and abandon those that do not.

Becoming a Better Professional

Freeman Tilden pointed out that love is the priceless ingredient in interpretation. If you are passionate about your chosen profession, that love shows through in all you say and do. That passion drives you to study the resource and the interpretive process throughout your career. You are continually seeking your own rewarding ways to get better at your craft in a lifelong journey of discovery and self-improvement.

You can never know enough. Your professional library is one important way for you to keep facts at your fingertips and cultivate new ideas and perspectives. We offer a brief bibliography of important books that you may want to include in your personal collection. The National Association for Interpretation also sells a *Bibliography of Interpretive Resources* (1998) that is updated every few years. It is a great reference to articles, web sites, and other resources you can put to work in your programs.

Professionalism will also involve you in professional meetings and training events. Make it a practice to attend one or more workshops or conferences each year. These opportunities for networking provide a chance to recharge your personal enthusiasm, collect new ideas, and make lifelong friends and professional contacts.

You can add additional certifications to your personal credentials through NAI. You might also decide you want a degree or advanced degree from a university. You can take travel-study tours in other countries to see how they approach interpretive activities. Visit other interpretive sites in your local area or region to learn from colleagues.

Among all of these, one of the greatest professional learning opportunities is to teach interpretation to others. Challenge yourself to make a presentation at a regional or national workshop in an area of personal expertise. Volunteer to be a guest presenter at local college classes on the subject of interpretation. Or become an NAI Certified Interpretive Trainer, sanctioned to teach the Certified Interpretive Guide course. You never learn so much as when you are challenged to teach others about your profession.

Reference Material
In addition to the six books already recommended for your basic interpretive resource library, we suggest the following:

Alderson, William T., and Shirley Paine Low. 1976. *Interpretation of Historic Sites.* Nashville, TN: American Association for State and Local History.

Edelstein, Daniel. 1990. *A Program Planner: For Naturalists and Outdoor Educators.* San Rafael, CA: Joy of Nature.

Grater, Russell K., and Earl Jackson, Eds. 1978. *The Interpreter's Handbook: Methods, Skills & Techniques.* Tucson, AZ: Southwest Parks and Monument Association.

Grinder, Alison L., and E. Sue McCoy. 1985. *The Good Guide: A Sourcebook for Interpreters, Docents and Tour Guides.* Scottsdale, AZ: Ironwood Press.

Gross, Michael, Ron Zimmerman, et al. The Interpreter's Handbook Series. Stevens Point, WI: UWSP Foundation Press, Inc.

Machlis, Gary E., and Donald R. Field, Eds. 1984. *On Interpretation: Sociology for Interpreters of Natural and Cultural History.* Corvallis, OR: Oregon State University Press.

National Park Service. 1996/2001. Interpretive Development Program Curriculum (www.nps.gov/idp/interp).

Tilden, Freeman. *The Fifth Essence: An Invitation to Share in Our Eternal Heritage.* Washington, DC: National Park Trust Fund Board.